Mindful & Intentional Money Management

PRAISE FOR
MINDFUL & INTENTIONAL MONEY MANAGEMENT

I propose that, for the vast majority of people, financial management is a challenge. Overall, most people did not intentionally set goals, receive any formal education in developing money management plans, or even feel comfortable engaging in those discussions. As a career educator, I often say, "We don't know what we have not been taught." Mistakes in financial decisions can negatively impact one for a lifetime. Many marriages have dissolved because of money mismanagement. Regardless of the amount of money one has, effective money management is beneficial for well-being in every aspect of life. There are prior wealthy people who could have retained or enhanced that wealth if only better fiscal decisions had been made. Regardless of a person's status of employment or net worth, topics addressed in *Mindful & Intentional Money Management* are useful over one's life span. Dr. Linda Simpson has provided us with a self-help book of collective, proactive, and personalized strategies to avoid the pitfalls of financial mismanagement. As a prior administrative supervisor of Dr. Simpson in higher education, I have personal knowledge of her decades of teaching consumer education and financial literacy. She is an expert in the field and uses innovative methods that are practical and inclusive of relevant information. Even after I moved to another university and was no longer Dr. Simpson's supervisor, I recruited her to teach an online consumer economics class and provide workshops for my faculty to develop an online financial literacy class. Dr. Simpson identifies strategies to engage the reader toward successful behavioral change, with the objective of moving from money mismanagement to effective money management. If there was ever a time we needed *Mindful & Intentional Money Management*, it is now.

—**Dr. Loretta P. Prater**, Dean (Retired),
Southeast Missouri State University

It was an honor to learn from Dr. Simpson. Her financial lessons and guidance in college and afterward launched me into the position I am in today. I owe a majority of my educational and financial success to her and would encourage others to learn from her as well. The next time I'm asked for financial advice, read *Mindful & Intentional Money Management* will be the words out of my mouth. It's a win-win!

—**Marissa Iles**, Former Student and Owner and
President at Magnificent M.Iles Events, LLC

As a professional colleague for nearly a decade, Linda has demonstrated a unique way of approaching personal financial management from a human perspective. She's been teaching the subject at the university level for quite some time and is a champion for the subject, creating a financial education center to provide support and expert advice for students. It's wonderful to see that she's formally publishing her unique approach to helping others take control of their finances!

—**Austin Cheney**, Dean of the College of Business,
Eastern Illinois University

Financial literacy can be intimidating and overwhelming, but Dr. Linda Simpson has a unique talent for breaking down complex concepts into easy-to-understand terms. Her passion for teaching along with her mentorship inspired me to think beyond the textbook and pursue a lifelong career as a finance professional. Dr. Simpson's newest project, *Mindful & Intentional Money Management*, is an invaluable resource for anyone looking to take control of their finances and build a solid foundation for their financial future.

—**Jackie Garren**, Former Student and Commercial Banker

As a K–12 teacher and administrator, I recognize the importance of financial literacy for all. *Mindful & Intentional Money Management* by Dr. Linda Simpson is a must-read for any individual seeking to gain control over their finances. Linda's expertise on financial literacy makes Linda's book not only easy to understand but easy to apply to your life and the lives of those around you. Overall, if you are seeking new and practical solutions to move from "chaos to calm" in your financial world, *Mindful & Intentional Money Management* provides a solid foundation and action steps to make it happen.

—**McLain Schaefer**, Director of LIFT (Leaders Innovating for Tomorrow), Former Elementary School Principal, High School Assistant Principal, and Classroom Educator

Mindful
— & —
Intentional
Money Management

AN UNBEATABLE SYSTEM
TO CALM THE CHAOS

Linda D. Simpson, PhD

NEW YORK
LONDON • NASHVILLE • MELBOURNE • VANCOUVER

Mindful & Intentional Money Management

AN UNBEATABLE SYSTEM TO CALM THE CHAOS

© 2024 Linda Simpson, PhD

Published in New York, New York, by Morgan James Publishing. Morgan James is a trademark of Morgan James, LLC. www.MorganJamesPublishing.com

Proudly distributed by Publishers Group West®

Morgan James BOGO™

A **FREE** ebook edition is available for you or a friend with the purchase of this print book.

CLEARLY SIGN YOUR NAME ABOVE

Instructions to claim your free ebook edition:
1. Visit MorganJamesBOGO.com
2. Sign your name CLEARLY in the space above
3. Complete the form and submit a photo of this entire page
4. You or your friend can download the ebook to your preferred device

ISBN 9781636982489 paperback
ISBN 9781636982496 ebook
Library of Congress Control Number: 2023939597

Cover Design by:
Andrew Averso
www.andrewaverso.com

Interior Design by:
Chris Treccani
www.3dogcreative.net

Morgan James is a proud partner of Habitat for Humanity Peninsula and Greater Williamsburg. Partners in building since 2006.

Get involved today! Visit: www.morgan-james-publishing.com/giving-back

Disclaimer

Because each person's situation is unique, the information provided in *Mindful and Intentional Money Management: An Unbeatable System to Calm the Chaos* is for informational purposes only and should not be considered as financial or investment advice. The author and publisher of this book are not licensed financial advisors, and the content of this book should not be interpreted as a recommendation or endorsement of any specific financial product or strategy.

The strategies, techniques, and concepts discussed in this book may not be suitable for everyone, as individual financial situations and goals vary. As such, the reader assumes full responsibility for their financial decisions. The reader also acknowledges that investing in financial markets involves inherent risks, past performance is not indicative of future results, and no guarantee of investment success is provided.

The examples provided in this book are for illustrative purposes only and should not be considered as guarantees of similar results. The reader should conduct their own research and due diligence before applying any of the concepts or strategies discussed.

By reading this book, the reader acknowledges and agrees to the above disclaimer and releases the author and publisher from any liability associated with the use or implementation of the information contained herein. Financial decisions must be made based on individual circumstances.

CONTENTS

ACKNOWLEDGMENTS

First and foremost, to my husband, Doug, for his love and support and for always believing in me.

To my daughters, Emily and Amelia, and my siblings, Carole, Donna, and Larry, for their excitement and support for my newest endeavor.

To my grandkids, Reya, Lincoln, Case, Georgia, and Stevie Jo. My legacy and future generation to become financially literate, set goals, and continue to instill sound money management skills in others.

To Nick, who I still say has the largest rolodex of anyone I know, for connecting me with the best of the best.

To Teresa, for connecting me with Nick.

To Catherine, for helping me edit the final draft of this book and prepare it for publishing.

To Jill, for inspiring me on this journey.

To my professional mentors, Loretta, Martha, Jayne, Gayle, and several others. I wouldn't be where I am today if not for each one of you.

And to my publisher, Morgan James Publishing, for helping me share this important message with people who need it.

ABOUT ANCHORD MONEY

Anchord is not a typo or misspelling but is a combination of two words: Anchor and Accord.

An anchor is a heavy object used to secure a vessel at sea. Water is unstable, like finances, and the anchor provides security. Accord is to bring into agreement and to be consistent or in harmony. Let's compare two money-related lifestyles: chaos and calm.

Money often creates chaos and impacts every facet of your life. A constant struggle with finances causes instability that results in uncertainty and upheaval. It prohibits you from having calmness or consistency in your life with the continual concern of paying your monthly bills and making ends meet.

Money dictates the lifestyle you live and many of your daily decisions. The effects of financial hardships can be felt not only by an individual, but can also impact marriages, families, and communities. You would be hard-pressed to find someone who doesn't need some or a lot of help with their finances.

Now turn that chaotic scenario around and picture calmness. The security of knowing that your monthly bills and unexpected expenses are covered, even with some money left over to secure your financial future. You now have some peace. I'm not saying that money buys happiness, but it can certainly make life easier to navigate.

Anchord Money was created to empower individuals and families with the knowledge and skills needed to foster their overall financial health. This is done by creating personalized plans based on an individual's conscious and unconscious money management behaviors. The curriculum is not a rigid, one-size-fits-all approach but rather it meets you where you are and encourages mindful, intentional decisions that fit your particular goals, habits, values, and lifestyle.

This program is *anchored* in a proven track record.

Secure / Safe / Anchor + Accord = Security and Peace

FOREWORD

Never make a promise without a plan.
—My father, Zig Ziglar

A t Ziglar, Inc., we have a seven-step goal-setting system to help individuals achieve the best. But if I had to change the name of this process, I would simply call it "How to get what you want."

Goals clarify what we want and show us where to get it. According to recent research, most people are not motivated just to achieve goals, but instead to solve problems. They like to tackle to-do lists instead of seeing progress rise on a goal. The seven-step goal-setting system does exactly that: identifies how to solve the problem.

The steps are

1. Write the goal down.
2. Write all the benefits of achieving the goal or solving the problem.
3. Include the obstacles in your way.
4. Determine the knowledge you need to gain.
5. Identify the people to help you.
6. Create a plan of action.
7. Set a date to achieve or solve the problem.

What problems are you facing today? Is it the problem of retiring comfortably? Of reducing the chaos in your financial life? Of building generational wealth? Regardless of your starting point, Linda Simpson's insights in these pages will help you get what you want.

As you'll soon uncover in the pages ahead, my father identified seven spokes on the wheel of life. One of them is financial, a crucial spoke that impacts all the rest. When I surveyed the field of financial literacy programs, however, I found a gaping hole in what they offered: they all went straight into specific tactics before tackling the why.

They don't ask you to take a step back at the beginning of the process and ask yourself what you want. That's why I love Linda's process; it begins with the why. If you don't have a solid why for moving from chaos to calm in your financial life, tactics won't help you. Jim Rohn said, "The stronger the why, the easier the how becomes."

My father also said, "If standard of living is your major objective, quality of life almost never improves. But if quality of life is your number one objective, standard of living almost always improves." Thanks to that bit of wisdom, I've developed a formula for balanced success in your career and financial life: quality of life = quality of work.

If you aim for quality of life in your personal, physical, family, mental, career, and spiritual lives, you'll find your finances improving as well. If you have balanced success in the other spokes, your money situation will be all right. You'll wake up one day and realize every minute has a purpose and every dollar has a plan.

There's an important caveat, however: It's easy to read these words and fail to internalize them. People almost never start thinking about money until they are captivated by a dream or devastated by a disaster. Unfortunately, for most, it's the latter.

Disaster has struck. The car is repossessed. You suddenly lose your job. You snap-to and realize you have a mountain of debt. Or you could start with the dream. Take the time at the outset to determine your ideal future and start working toward it.

The funny thing is, you'll probably have the same goals, tactics, and actions in either case. It's just that those motivated by disaster will be stressed out through the process, and those motivated by the dream will instead feel joy and gratitude. So don't wait.

Now, I'm not saying we can determine our future 100 percent. Life may bless us with an unexpected child or an unexpected car breakdown. Instead of attempting to control the future, we need to control our habits. Because our habits determine our future. Dad liked to say, "The number one reason people do not achieve their goals is because they trade what they want most for what they want now." Disciplined habits do the opposite.

For most of us, this begins with taking our bad habits and replacing them with good ones. We might have to dig ourselves out of a hole over time. We may need to cut down on our spending drastically. Regardless, when we take itty-bitty bad habits and slowly replace them with itty-bitty good ones, it will alter the landscape of our lives. If you do this long enough, you'll see a shift in your family legacy.

Yes, it's good to leave an inheritance for our children and grandchildren. But what if we left them a deeper legacy than that? What if our children were financially literate, knew how to set goals, and had good financial habits long after we are gone?

You have the opportunity to shift the trajectory of generations with what you're about to read. Not only will Linda teach you how to set goals, focus on tiny habits, and keep the why in front of you, but you'll also learn how to equip the people around you and generations to come with how to do the same thing.

Let me leave you with this quote from my father, on the lighter side: "In life, I've had problems when I've had money. I've had problems when I haven't had money. And all in all, when you have problems, it's better to have money."

Linda will not solve all your problems, but she'll show you a way to have problems and have money. That will make your life easier and help you achieve the best. I'm excited for you to begin this journey.

-**Tom Ziglar**
CEO of Ziglar, Inc. and Proud Son
of American Legend Zig Ziglar
Ziglar.com

PREFACE

Thank you for joining me on this journey. The fact that you are seeking resources to improve your financial situation means you have some level of commitment to seek a more positive future. I commend you for that. I hope that you find the content of this book helpful in moving from chaos to calm in your finances.

I want to tell you why I wrote this book. Since 1994, I have taught financial literacy to children, teenagers, young adults, and older adults. In other words, I've dedicated my entire professional life to helping people learn about money management. Time and time again, I've seen people struggle, and it has created compassion in me to help people work through challenging financial situations.

I want to help you too. If you can just follow this plan and develop mindful and intentional money habits, your financial situation will significantly improve. This will, in turn, have a positive impact on your life. By reading this book, you'll get

- Empowerment to become your best financial self
- A foundation that can strengthen your family and community in a domino effect
- Research-based information instead of anecdotes

- Multiple opportunities to engage with the content and make it personal to you
- A basic, nonintimidating process for financial success
- A plan that fits with your habits, personality, attitudes, and values rather than a cookie-cutter approach that's been built for someone else
- A custom financial strategy that leads to increased income, reduced expenses, paid-off debt, appreciating assets, and growing net worth
- A skill set to teach your children, or other young people in your life, how to develop their money management skills

I also want you to know that you're not alone when you finish this book. I don't want to make you motivated to change only to leave you without support. So I've built many other options to help you along the way after our journey through this book is finished. They include the following:

- Audio lectures with Companion Guides to walk you through the process step by step. The Companion Guides provide thought questions and hands-on activities that challenge you to think deeper about your personal money management behaviors. You will put what you learn into action that is relevant to your financial situation.
- Parent's Guides, downloadable PDFs, resources, and digital tools that help you with your personal financial planning as well as strategies to teach others how to develop sound financial skills.
- Virtual curriculum that can be completed at your own pace.
- Multiple opportunities for engaging one on one and in communities.

- Support and relationship building through blogs, podcasts, and digital communities.

By embarking on this journey, your life, and your family's life, can change forever. When you build a financial plan around *your* value system, you will stick with it. Life is tough, and it throws us many curveballs—if you can eliminate one of those struggles that are often related to finances, you will not only survive but thrive.

But for any of this to succeed, I need a commitment from you. For the content of this book to work, you must commit to change, develop new money habits, learn something new, and devote time and energy to improving your financial situation. I can't give you a magic pill that fixes everything, but I can give you tried-and-true methods that will get you to your financial goals if you're willing to do your part.

While you will see immediate results with small changes, this overall process will take time; it's a journey, not a destination. Hands-on activities will allow you to put what you learn into action that is relevant to your personal financial situation. You will think big and dream about your financial future, evaluate your current financial situation, and fill in the gaps between the two. My goal for you is to develop muscle memory that will automate your financial planning. You will move from being reactive and in money chaos to proactive and calm.

This process will challenge you to take a hard look at your current financial situation. You may find this difficult, but it is absolutely necessary to get from where you are now to where you want to be in the future. **Mindful** and **intentional** are two key terms that I will focus on throughout this book. Financial planning, decisions, and purchases are often made mindlessly, without us even thinking about them. Being intentional will make you more aware when making these decisions. In the end, it will be worth it, as you move from chaos to calm with your money management.

Are you ready to get started?

INTRODUCTION

On the first day of class each semester, a hand goes up, and the same question is asked by a student: "Do I need to be good at math to do well in this course?" My response: "Absolutely not." While a few basic math skills are necessary, pretty much any financial question can be answered via Google or Siri, or online financial calculators are available to make the process easier. The bottom line is, financial planning is intimidating, and it doesn't have to be. While there's a place for fancy calculators in the finance world, that does not mean that one is required to create your personal financial plan. With that, many times, the topic is avoided because you feel overwhelmed and don't know how to get started.

> The small investment of this book will help you reduce stress by allowing you to build a solid financial future— moving from chaos to calm. That's what I call an excellent return on investment (ROI).

Does this sound like you? Let's reduce those concerns, so you can feel confident in creating a personalized financial plan that works for you *and* one that you can stick with.

A problem with some financial plans is that they're overcomplicated. While financial advisors can help you, they're not necessary for getting started. At this point, you do not need a complicated, multipage plan that requires a graduate degree in finance to understand, thus making this topic more intimidating to you. Down the road, as you become more comfortable and confident with your finances, these professionals would be helpful. At this time, you just need to take smaller, simpler steps to get started building a plan that fits your needs and lifestyle. Otherwise, you won't stick to it.

Another concern with some financial planners or coaches is they tell you where you should and should not spend your money. Do you really think that this cookie-cutter "perfect" financial plan will work for you if things that you enjoy or find important are eliminated from your life? Probably not! While their plan will allow you to become a millionaire in twenty years, it might require you to drink only tap water and cook all meals at home for those twenty years. That's not realistic and is no way to live. You will likely not stick with it.

I am a firm believer that you must build a financial plan around *your* habits, personality, attitudes, and values—and what *you* feel is important. Think about it: Spinach is healthy, and a nutritionist may advise you to eat it . . . but if you don't like it, you won't eat it. It's the same way with money management; if you don't like it, you won't stick with it.

Managing money is a learning process. It takes practice to do it well. No one is, and you will never be, perfect at managing your money, for several reasons. Life happens, you may get sick, so you need to pivot and make changes in your occupation, savings and investment strategies, retirement goals, etc. Circumstances may happen that are out of your control. The stock market goes down; interest rates go up. The list goes on and on. So positioning yourself with the financial knowledge and skill set will better prepare you to get through those unexpected situations.

We all make mistakes with our money. You have made mistakes and will make future mistakes. Even the most financially successful people do. Just google "worst Warren Buffett investments." He's one of the most financially successful people of all time, with access to more information about investing than almost anyone in the world. And he still makes mistakes. Thus, the key to financial success is not to avoid mistakes; it's to reduce mistakes, learn from your mistakes, and keep moving forward. Simply being more mindful and intentional with your money is your starting point. And that's exactly what I'm going to help you do.

I've been teaching financial literacy since 1994 in a variety of situations and through different platforms, such as face-to-face and online classrooms, webinars, workshops, conference presentations, etc. During that time, I've helped thousands of people of all ages and life stages to set goals and create simple financial plans. It doesn't take a financial wizard to build a solid, basic financial foundation, nor does it require you to have a high income. It's about being more mindful and intentional and making some necessary adjustments to your spending and saving habits.

I encourage you to visit my website at Anchord.money for access to valuable resources to further expand your learning. Online courses are available that include audio lectures, along with Companion Guides. A special section for parents includes a curriculum to teach children, aged preschool through high school, about money. Audio lectures, workbooks, and a Parent Guide are included with each program.

Building a Solid Financial Foundation

Three action plans and commitment are what it takes to build a solid financial foundation: know where you're going, know where you are, and learn, plan, and execute.

First, you need to know where you're going. If you are heading out on a long trip, do you just jump in the car and take off without a map or navigation system in hand? Of course not! Then why would you want to do that with your financial future?

I often ask my young audience members, "When do you want to retire?" The most common response is fifty years old because eighteen- to twenty-year-olds think that's really old, and they think that they will be over the hill at that age. Then I ask, "How do you plan to get there?" They don't have a clue and haven't even thought about it. I tell them, "If fifty is your goal, you can start working and planning now on reaching that goal, rather than waiting until you are forty-five years old. By then, it's too late."

Second, it takes knowing where you are right now in terms of your income, assets, expenses, debt, and net worth. This gives you a snapshot of your current financial picture today: the good, the bad, and the ugly. Don't worry if it's more bad and ugly than good right now. Most people, including my husband and me, have had life stages when their finances weren't too pretty. In fact, while you and I would both likely prefer to have no bad or ugly parts of our finances, those experiences actually present great opportunities for us to grow and learn from our mistakes.

Third, you need to learn, plan, and execute a personal financial plan. This includes understanding the plan and why it is significant to you. Learn why each piece of the plan exists and how it helps you achieve your goals. It will help you make decisions as you execute your plan *and* forge a deeper emotional connection to your actions. Small, simple steps will lead you closer to the life and financial goals you want to achieve.

Know where you're going, know where you are, then learn, plan, and execute. Follow these three action plans to reach your destination. But first, I want to discuss a topic that is important in your finances:

Simplify, Simplify, Simplify

You may be thinking, *I bought this book to learn how to create a financial plan and here she is, telling me that I need to simplify my life.* Hang with me. Once you dig through the personal process of uncluttering your life, you will understand.

From every angle, modern life encourages us to do more, be more, achieve more, and spend more. We end up trying to do "all the things" and then wonder why we feel tired, stressed out, or stuck on autopilot as one day drifts into the next. Getting in autopilot mode will be your worst enemy when trying to make changes and plan for the future. You are in survival mode, being reactive to all situations and constantly trying to keep up or catch up.

That's why it's so important to **simplify**.

Simplify your finances. This will make it easier to keep on top of how much you're spending each month and avoid the buildup of stacks of paper and forgotten bills to pay. Set up automations, such as bill/debt payments, savings, and investments. Enter all bill due dates on your calendar to avoid late payments. Create a simplified monthly budget that works for you. Then, you can focus your time and energy elsewhere.

Other areas to simplify that directly relate to your financial picture include the following:

- **Your meals**. Make a weekly meal plan and use that to make a shopping list to remain within your food budget. Plan ahead so you can avoid eating out.
- **Your clothes**. Purge your closet and earn a bit of money by selling clothes you don't wear. Plus, you can select which clothes to wear in advance of your week, and perhaps purchase basic items that will round out your wardrobe.
- **Your time**. Become mindful of your time, the time you spend and the time you waste. Learn to say "No" to things that don't align with your priorities. Take a step back and think about your priorities.
- **Your paper clutter**. Invest in a simple filing system and use clearly labeled dividers to organize everything. If you don't need a paper copy, scan it, and save it digitally. If you don't need it at all, throw it away.
- **Your home**. A cluttered home prevents you from relaxing and recharging. You are surrounded by chaos. Create space in your home and make it easier for you to manage.

My father passed away in 2022, my husband's mom passed away a year earlier, and his brother passed away in 2014. They were all pack rats; I've never seen so much *stuff* in my life. We had to go through it all deciding what to keep, sell, pitch, or donate—and we still have a room full of photo albums of people we don't know, letters from the 1970s to our loved ones from people we don't know, keepsakes, and so on. As time goes on, we are able to go through and pitch a little more. Our experience opened our eyes to realize that we don't want to do that to our own kids.

Now we look around at our stuff and think, *Will our kids want this?* rather than, *Do I (or we) want this?* We still have a long way to go with minimizing, but we are aware that it needs to be done.

Simplifying reduces stress and declutters your space and mind. You can focus on what's important to you. It's about finding easier ways to do the things you have to do and giving yourself more time to do the things you want to do.

[Use the Companion Guide to develop strategies on how you can simplify your life.]

Now we are going to dive into the three action plans: know where you're going, know where you are, then learn, plan, and execute. First, we'll talk about knowing where you're going.

ANCHORD MONEY

Part 1:

KNOW WHERE YOU'RE GOING

am going to use the road trip across the country example again. You make sure the car is tuned up and fueled up, you have enough snacks, and your music playlist (or audiobooks) is ready to go. What's the final piece of the puzzle? A good map or navigation system. You'll never make it to your destination without a good map. You plan, plan, plan for this trip that may last one or two weeks, so why wouldn't you create a plan for something that impacts your entire life?

Living life day to day without dreaming about your financial future is the same idea. That's why we're starting with the concept of setting goals. Take a moment to think: Where do you want to be financially five years from now? What about ten? What about twenty?

While that seems a long time away, thinking about your goals now will help you get there. Goals serve as your road map in life, helping you visualize your desired destination. They serve as written statements about what a person (or family) wants or needs to accomplish. Goals can help you move from chaos to calm by having a plan, thus creating more peace in your life. If you want to reach your financial goals, now is the time to make plans related to all the financial aspects of your life, even retirement.

Goals help you stay focused and on target. People get extremely busy with day-to-day activities and oftentimes confuse this busyness with progress or productivity. Busyness does not equal productiveness. Step back and examine your daily activities and distractions. Note how much time is wasted on trivial things, such as social media, compared to how much time is spent on true productivity. The goal-setting process helps you focus on being productive to reach your desired result.

Next, we are going to break down goal setting into three sections: money habits, eight areas of your life, and setting SMARTER goals. This process will help you to determine where you're going.

CHAPTER 1:

Money Habits

———

About twenty years ago, a nurse in our community called me; I'll refer to her as "Julie." The reason that I share her profession is because you can tell that she had a solid income, especially for our community. I could sense from her voice that she was upset. She was in a financial bind, and even worse, her husband knew nothing about it. She called because a former student of mine suggested that she contact me.

When I asked Julie to explain her situation to me, what she revealed wasn't a pretty picture. She had maxed out all her credit cards, putting herself into a significant amount of debt with high interest rates. To make ends meet, she had made multiple visits to a payday loan company. Hearing this immediately signaled red flags to me about how desperate her situation had become.

Julie was overwhelmed by the time she reached out to me, feeling as if she was backed into a corner and couldn't get out. It's not that she didn't make good money. She had the kind of career that would make you assume she had a good financial picture. But her spending and accumulated debt had begun to *heavily* outpace her income. Adding to the stress was the fact that she had hidden this financial information from her husband.

As you may have experienced in your own life, money issues and relationship issues frequently overlap, and Julie was no different. The temptation to hide our financial picture—especially when it's not a pretty picture—from our spouse or significant other, parents, and other family members is common. This is a warning sign that things are not right, either in your financial world or with your relationship, and sometimes both. This situation can trigger intense emotions and stress.

Desperate for a solution, Julie asked me what she could do to recover from her financial mistakes. As I asked a few more questions, I began to understand that she was looking "to fix" the wrong thing. She was asking for a quick fix to her debt when what she really needed was a long-term solution that would get her out and keep her out of her current financial situation. In other words, "nurse Julie" was asking for a Band-Aid for a wound that was already deeply infected.

She had many underlying issues causing her irrational spending behaviors. Unless she addressed those issues, any "solution" would be temporary. She might get out of debt or into a better debt situation than her piles of credit card and payday loan debt, but within weeks or months, she'd likely be in the exact same financial position if she didn't get to the root cause of the problem.

This is an extreme example of how habits and dealing with emotions through spending can have a negative impact on finances. These emotions need to be addressed before we can begin working and building new habits to plan our financial future. Again, you may be thinking, *Here she is again, wanting me to dig deep into my*

emotions when all I want is to learn how to create a financial plan.
Trust me, you will be much more successful in sticking with a plan
by working through this process.

There are hands-on exercises in this section that require some
critical thinking, so don't feel that you need to work through them
all in one day. Don't make this an overwhelming activity. It's not
a race; it's a journey.

Next, we will look at the biggest contributors to your financial behavior that have nothing to do with your income, where
you live, or your investment returns. These include money scripts,
personality, habits, values, and attitudes, which have a significant
impact on your financial planning and behaviors. Getting to the
"why" of your spending behavior is just as important as crunching
the income, expenses, and debt numbers. We could work with
numbers all day long, but if we don't focus on the reasons behind
those numbers, we're wasting a lot of time. Let's take a closer look
at each one.

Money Scripts

Whether you know it or not, you have developed what are called
money scripts. These are long-held beliefs and perspectives
on money that you have learned throughout your life. Some
money scripts are helpful, but others may hinder you. Your
home environment and how your parent(s) handled money
have a significant impact on you. For example, if your family
lived paycheck to paycheck, there may have been much money-
related anxiety. That has an impact on your current relationship
with money. It's important to be aware of your money scripts
and evaluate those that have a negative impact but embrace the
positive scripts that help you move forward.

It's so interesting to hear class discussions when students share their money experiences growing up. Throughout the semester, I can tell students who have had sound financial management skills instilled in them. Hands are raised, and the students say, "My dad said" or "My mom said . . ." Their responses are often spot on. On the flip side, I have students taking my course materials and sharing them with their parents to use. Their goal is to not struggle financially like they witnessed their parents doing while growing up. At this point, their money scripts have been formed.

What money scripts come to mind from when you were growing up?

Determine which scripts have a positive or negative impact on your current spending behavior.

[Use the Companion Guide to further reflect on your money scripts and the positive or negative impact on your current spending behavior.]

Personality

Personality also plays a major role in your financial behaviors. It is useful to understand the various money personalities when finding the right approach to investing, spending, saving, and the overall management of your finances. Five common money personalities are investors, savers, big spenders, debtors, and shoppers. Look at your siblings or other family members, and you will be able to identify a variety of money personalities, even though you grew up in the same household.

Money personalities aren't good or bad. They aren't right or wrong. In fact, anyone can become financially successful, no matter what their natural money personality is. Knowing your tendencies is key.

Personality impacts people at all levels of wealth too. For example, I recently connected with Russ Alan Prince, executive director of Private Wealth magazine and chief content officer for High-Net-Worth Genius, about the different types of personalities displayed by the ultra-wealthy. Mr. Prince consults with family offices, the wealthy, fast-tracking entrepreneurs, and select professionals. He is one of the most knowledgeable people in the world when it comes to serving wealthy people. (And I might be selling him short.)

According to Mr. Prince, high-net-worth people typically display one or more of the following nine personalities:

1. **Family Stewards:** People who are motivated by the need to protect their families over the long term.

2. **Phobics:** People who—although they are wealthy—dislike thinking about money.

3. **Independents:** People whose primary objective in accumulating wealth is to achieve financial independence and the accompanying security.

4. **Anonymous:** People typified by their deep-seated—and sometimes irrational—need for privacy and confidentiality in all of their financial dealings, as well as selected personal dealings.

5. **Moguls:** People who are motivated to accumulate more and more wealth in order to achieve personal power (and, by extension, influence, if not control).

6. **VIPs:** People who are motivated to accumulate assets and use their wealth, in part to achieve greater status and prestige.

7. **Accumulators:** People who seek to accumulate wealth out of an overriding concern for personal financial well-being.

8. **Gamblers:** People who believe their skills and competence will protect them from all significant threats.
9. **Innovators:** People who believe their analytical capabilities will sustain them and protect them from external threats.

Although Mr. Prince focuses on the ultra-wealthy, these personalities are not unique to the super-rich. As you read through them, consider whether any of Mr. Prince's types or the five I mentioned above feel like you. You might find that you resonate with more than one personality type.

[Use the Companion Guide to examine which personality you can most identify with.]

Now that we've talked about money scripts and personality, let's examine our personal habits, values, and attitudes. All three of these play a key role in your spending behavior. They need to be aligned with our spending behavior, which should, in turn, align with our goals.

We'll break it down into the following sections:

1. Aligning Habits and Money
2. Aligning Attitudes and Money
3. Aligning Values and Money

Aligning Habits and Money

Habits are things you do mindlessly that impact your money and are a collection of all the years you've spent so far doing what you're doing. If you don't change your habits, then no lasting change in your financial situation will occur. Factors that have helped you form these habits are your money scripts, values, and attitudes toward money.

Emotional habits have also been formed that cause us to buy things we don't need or want only because of a certain emotion or mood that we feel at that time. Changing this behavior must be intentional to stop the mindless spending.

We often spend money mindlessly because that's what we learned, have always done, and have never even considered that it's a bad habit we should stop or change.

Thankfully, those habits can be rewired to give you the kinds of results you want. But first, it requires understanding our money scripts, personality, and values—and how they drive our habits. This shows us how money impacts the most important areas of our lives and gives us the perspective we need to make changes.

[Use the Companion Guide to identify purchases that you make regularly without thinking. Then calculate the cost of how much you spend on these purchases.]

Money Habits, Marriage, and Parenting with Jamie Nichols

Jamie Nichols is a middle-market commercial banker at one of the nation's largest financial institutions. She serves businesses that generate $20 million to $500 million in revenue each year with financial services and strategy, helping them grow while managing investments and risks. Her journey into the financial industry began when she pursued a bachelor's degree in Family Consumer Sciences, and then became one of my graduate assistants while earning her master's degree.

Jamie identifies as a classic saver. She manages her finances and investments tightly and loves teaching her children about financial literacy. This money script and personality comes from her upbringing and career in the financial industry. On the other hand, her husband is a spender. He grew up in a financially unstable family, as the child of two immigrants living in New York. He made it through boarding school and college by getting scholarships and got a high-paying job right out of college.

Because of his upbringing and career, his money scripts are different. He wants to give his and Jamie's children everything he never had growing up. These different money habits have led to marital conflict: she loves budgets and savings, reducing exposure to interest, and living beneath her means, while her husband loves to spend, give big gifts, and enjoy luxuries now.

Most married people will fall into one of these two categories, to varying degrees. There are multiple ways to overcome these challenges, but they ultimately come down to communication and consistency. Some couples will combine their finances, talk through their money habits, get on the same page with a budget, and work through it every week. Other couples will keep their finances largely separate, splitting and sharing expenses and using disposable income how they each wish. This is the strategy Jamie and her husband use, and it works for them.

Then come the expenses associated with kids themselves. This includes childcare, clothes, food, and all the sports and extracurricular programs. All in all, children are often the biggest line item on any couple's budget, especially if the parents both work and need formal childcare. Jamie explained to me that it takes a village, and a lot of careful money management, to take care of the kids.

In the midst of this, how does Jamie pass on her strength of financial management to her children? She says that a child is never too young to learn basic financial literacy. She gives them money for doing their chores and encourages them to think about what they want to do with that money. If they're at the store, then she will point out their favorite items and the prices and let the kids plan how they want to spend. This led to her son deciding to pass on buying his favorite trading cards when he learned that a pack costs $25.

When her son got a bit older, she also gave him his own debit card. He can keep track of his balance using an app on his iPad, so even as a child, he learns how to track his expenses and manage his money. Jamie also talks to her kids about their college savings account and what that means.

Her biggest tip for teaching financial literacy? Make it fun. You can play games with your children that involve earning and managing money, like Monopoly and The

Game of Life. Without even knowing it, your children can learn concepts like opportunity cost and investment.

Next, we will look at how we can align our attitudes and money.

Aligning Attitudes and Money

Everyone has a slightly different attitude toward money. Some people have an attitude of scarcity, and others have an attitude of abundance (or even overabundance). This impacts money spending behaviors. For example, someone with a relaxed attitude might make a hasty decision to make a big purchase that leads them into debt. Work through this first exercise to understand your money attitudes. Your responses may reveal thoughts and attitudes that you weren't aware of in relation to money.

Exercise #1: General Attitude toward Money

This activity will clarify your general attitude toward money.[1] When paired with your values, which I will help you do below, it gives you the foundation you need for understanding your habits. For this one, all you do is circle or highlight the "Yes" or the "No."

1. No matter how much money I have, I feel like I need more. Yes/No
2. It bugs me when I learn I could have bought the same thing for less money elsewhere. Yes/No
3. Money serves as the ultimate success indicator. Yes/No
4. Not having enough money makes me anxious. Yes/No
5. I frequently dream of being a millionaire. Yes/No

---

1 Adapted from a circular by Debra Pankow, former family economic specialist, North Dakota State University, 2003.

6. It's difficult for me to spend money for any reason. Yes/No
7. I frequently worry about having "enough" when I retire. Yes/No
8. I let money control my activities and behaviors. Yes/No
9. Money mattered to me even when I was a child. Yes/No
10. I often complain about the costs of products, even if only to myself. Yes/No

Now simply count the number of "Yes" responses. The higher the number, the more you value money. Pay attention to your score. A high number of "Yes" responses could mean you operate from a mindset of scarcity, that money makes you anxious and upset, and/or that you seek to save as much as you can. On the other hand, a high number of "No" responses could mean you are cavalier in your approach to money, that you don't think about it as much, and/or that you spend mindlessly.

[Use the Companion Guide to complete this exercise related to attitudes and money.]

Again, the results of this exercise and the next two that you will complete will affect the financial goals you set. You want your values, attitudes, and goals to align because it will increase your chances of success.

Aligning Values and Money

Core values are the priorities you prize most in your life. These could include family, meaningful work, or giving back to your community. Core values are not possessions, activities, or experiences; they are aspects of defining yourself as a person. They bring about the most positive impact on your life. That is why it is essential to ensure that you are considering your values and what you want out of life when creating your financial plan.

We all have personal values that come from our relationships, influences, education, and life experiences. Do you know yours? Have you ever sat down to define your money values? More importantly, do your spending actions reflect those values?

When someone is dissatisfied with their financial situation, it may be because there is no alignment between their actions and values. Money is a vehicle to get what they want. They spend—most likely impulsively—based on current emotions, feelings, or societal pressure, instead of spending money—mindfully and intentionally—on the things that matter most to them.

If you value being debt-free, your actions must reflect it. You can't state a value of being debt-free and then overextend your credit by purchasing trivial items. At least, not if you want satisfaction in your financial life. It will come to a point where your reality comes into conflict with your stated values. This gives you what psychologists call cognitive dissonance, mental distress caused by this disconnect between two previously held beliefs.

This isn't about right or wrong. We each have our own goals and mindsets when it comes to finances. My role isn't to tell you what you "should" or "must" do, but rather help you clarify your personal goals and help you achieve them.

For example, if you find through the exercises outlined below that you spend too much money on things that don't matter to you, you can decide to change. By adopting better habits and being intentional, you can master how to align your values with your money.

To get a picture of your values and money, we will work through two more exercises:

- Prioritizing areas of your life that money most influences and why, and

- Selecting "this or that" between a set of two products, indicating which one you prefer.

Exercise #2: Prioritizing Areas of Life

This is a three-step exercise meant to help you determine your financial values.

[Use the Companion Guide to complete the following exercises to help you determine your financial values.]

Step 1: Make a List

Money impacts most areas of your life. Write down the areas of your life that money influences the most. Stick to the top five to seven areas. This will help in the next step.

Some examples might include the following:
- Lifestyle
- Marriage
- Parenting & Family
- Career
- Friendships
- Health
- Hobbies & Fun
- Education
- Giving
- Retirement

Step 2: Prioritize Your List

Now, rank your list in order of importance. Decide the top three to five priorities here. Prioritizing further clarifies your values and begins to show you the areas you need to invest money and time into.

Step 3: Know Your Why

Lastly, answer the following questions: Why are the values you selected important to you? Why do they matter? Dig deep and get answers. Again, give some thought to this. If you need to stop and think for a while, that's fine.

Understanding the "why" will help you remain motivated and inspire you to take action. You'll have the emotions attached to your values and decisions, which will fuel action. It will help you navigate difficult decisions and days when you're tired and want to ditch the plan.

Take the idea of the optimized retirement plan. The "why" here could be so that you can spend time with your children and grandchildren without having to worry about travel expenses or continue working into an advanced age.

The purpose of money here isn't simply to grow a huge 401(k). It runs deeper than that. You want to be able to invest in the relationships that matter most, create memories, and leave a legacy to be remembered. That's a good "why."

If you're having trouble coming up with your "why," here are a few prompts that could help:

- Security and peace of mind
- Freedom and choices
- Enrichment and fulfillment
- Knowledge and wisdom
- Legacy and inheritance
- Health and wellness
- Relationships and intimacy
- Independence and self-competence
- Responsibility and duty
- Generosity and charity

Take the time to determine the "why" underneath your values. These are big ideas, deep values that flow as an undercurrent beneath your day-to-day actions. We need to discover what they are and make sure your stated values align with your money behaviors.

Let's look at an example.

If one of your top values is parenting and family, your "why" might be building security and establishing a legacy and inheritance. Understanding this allows you to use money as a tool to focus on your priorities and values.

Building security could mean establishing an emergency fund, beginning long-term investments, and leveraging savings for a stable financial foundation.

Establishing a legacy could mean beginning a trust or providing for your descendant's education.

Deepening relationships could mean budgeting for immediate needs along with meaningful memories like vacations and quality time spent together.

See how clarifying our "why" affects our money behaviors?

Exercise #3: This or That

As I mentioned earlier, if you want to see someone's true values, take a look at their checkbook or transaction history. Your money will flow toward your values.

Now let's dial in and take a closer look at your financial values. To do that, follow this exercise.[2]

Imagine you get an unexpected windfall. You don't need this money for any of your expenses, so you're free to spend it on whatever you like. Listed below are several sets of this or that items to

---

2   Adapted from the High School Financial Planning Program (NEFE@), 1992.

spend that money on, and you must make one choice out of each pair. Simply circle or highlight your selection:

Note: This is an example of an exercise I use to help people identify their financial values by choosing between two options. The image below shows you what it looks like. [You can find the full version of it in your Companion Guide.]

This	That
Charitable Giving (e.g., church)	Vacation/Travel
Personal Appearance (e.g., clothes)	Charitable Giving
Social Activities (e.g.. eating out)	House (e.g., dream/vacation home)
Investments (e.g., retirement)	Hobbies (e.g.. sports)

Now, total the number of times you circled/highlighted each item in the activity:

- Car:
- Charitable Giving:
- Education:
- Hobbies:
- House:
- Personal Appearance:
- Investments:
- Social Activities:
- Vacation/Travel:

As I mentioned earlier, if you want to see someone's true values, take a look at their checkbook or transaction history. Your money will flow toward your values.

Revealing Your Money Values

If you're struggling to identify your money values or want to validate what you identified in the two exercises, this process can help.

The exercises may have shown a discrepancy between your stated values and your real actions. It also may have revealed uncomfortable information about your habits and attitude. This is a guilt-free zone. It's okay if you feel like you haven't made the progress you wanted up to this point. Now you know, and you can begin aligning your values and your habits and find yourself making progress toward your goals.

The following steps will increase your awareness as to what you have actually been spending money on. This is a good indication of your money values when you are not being as intentional and mindful as you will be moving forward. Then, over the next couple of chapters, I'll show you how to set goals that you can feel good about and actually achieve.

[Use the Companion Guide to increase your awareness of where your money goes.]

To fully reveal your money values, complete the following steps:

1. Go Over Your Bank and Credit Card Statements

Examine your transaction history via your bank and credit card statements for the last year. This gives a zoomed-out perspective on your money values and how well it aligns with your stated values. As you do this, does anything stick out? Do you see a pattern or imbalance? If so, don't worry. Recognizing the issue is the first step toward a solution.

2. Look at Your Budget

What is a budget except a spending plan based on your priorities? Take a look at your plan. If you don't have a fully formed budget yet don't worry either. We'll go over how to determine your income and expenses in the next section. The amount of money you have planned for a certain thing shows you how much you value it. In your budget, does your money currently serve the purpose you want it to?

3. Examine Your Lifestyle

Now, look at the house you live in, vehicles you own, grocery stores you shop at, hobbies, and everything else you use and spend time on. Money influences them all to a degree. Do these expenses line up with your stated values?

4. Determine a Change to Make

Look at your transactions, budget, and lifestyle. This will show you your money values more clearly. You'll also see a connection or disconnect between your money and your values. If you see a disconnect, then plan to make a single change. It doesn't have to be drastic or world-shaking. In fact, it should be a small, simple adjustment that builds momentum for the future.

5. Begin Living Out Your Values

Your values are your compass on the journey. If you're ever unsure where to turn, look at the compass. Live out your values by consistently referring to them when you make decisions regarding money. Before you spend, ask yourself

- Does this decision line up with my stated values?
- Will this decision get me closer to my goals?
- Am I on track to achieve my goals?

[Use the Companion Guide to help you reveal your values.]

You Can Do This

I know this chapter threw a lot of deep questions that required critical thinking. It may have pointed to uncomfortable truths, but hopefully, it motivated you to make a change. You might even be looking at your financial situation and feeling doubtful that you can ever get where you want to go. Before we move on, I want to reiterate that this is possible for you. You don't need to be a financial planner or math genius to become more mindful and intentional with your money. It takes small steps done consistently over time to reach your destination.

When my husband and I were first married in the early 1980s, we lived paycheck to paycheck. I say that, but often our minimal paychecks didn't even cover our spending to make it to the next paycheck. We had no financial goals, just like many people who may have picked up this book. We spent very little money back then because we simply didn't have it. I remember cutting pictures out of magazines and putting them into $1 frames to use for our home decor—so that we'd at least have something on our walls. I know what it's like to not have money.

We're in a much healthier financial situation now, and I get joy out of helping others. I often get emails from former students asking me to send them PowerPoint slides I used during my lectures. The most commonly requested one is my housing lecture. They are now at a time in their life when they are buying a home, so the topic is much more relevant to them. So they want to brush up on the content by relistening to my lectures.

In another situation, one of my colleagues conducted a peer evaluation on one of my lectures, and housing just happened to be the topic for that day. She had lived in the community for ten years and had always rented. After my lecture, she had the confidence to pursue buying a home! She said that she didn't know where to start, but again, I broke it down into simple steps. I even sent the presentation to my daughter before she and her husband bought their first home. How cool is that? And these are just the stories that I know about. Buying a home is such an overwhelming and stressful decision because, face it, it is likely the most expensive purchase that you will make throughout your lifetime. But just knowing and understanding the language used by real estate agents and loan institutions can provide the confidence to move forward.

Again, money doesn't buy happiness. It does, however, reduce stress and make life much easier to navigate. My goal for you is to have a reliable process in place to move toward your goals and turn your chaos into calm. If I can do it and have helped plenty of others do it, then I can help you too.

Chapter Summary

Money habits affect your money behaviors. We worked in this chapter to determine our money scripts, personality, habits, attitude, and values. This gives us the foundation we need to move forward. There are no wrong values or habits; it's more about alignment between them. With this information, we have an idea of where we are now and where we might want to go soon.

 | **KEY TAKEAWAYS**

- You are now aware of your money scripts, personality, values, and attitude.
- You have a clearer understanding of how your habits, attitudes, and values affect your spending. Think about one negative impact these have on your spending habits and how you can change it.

- Creating a mindful and intentional approach to money management is essential to making positive changes in your financial situation.

CHAPTER 2:

Eight Areas of Life

Whew, that last chapter was a heavy one that required a lot of processing and deep thought. This chapter is going to continue that challenge to better position yourself in setting your goals.

Have you ever felt like you've really got it going in one area of your life, things are clicking, all wheels are moving in the same direction? But in another area, it's chaos? Chaos is not fun, so you just avoid that area. It's overwhelming, and you don't want to deal with it. You can ride that train down that track, and everything will work for a while, but eventually, the tracks will likely start crisscrossing, possibly derailing the train.

Taking a closer look at all areas of your life and creating balance is essential. To do this, you need to do some more self-evaluation—where you are and where you want to be—and set specific goals in that area. Even if you have done nothing toward reaching that goal, having an action plan in place will significantly help.

Without goals, it's like running on a treadmill as fast as you can and not going anywhere. Tremendous effort is exerted, but it doesn't get you closer to where you want to go. You feel like you want to get somewhere, but you don't know where or what you want to achieve.

The solution? Setting the right goals that are personal to you. We just discussed the idea of aligning your habits, values, and attitudes with money. Goals should follow this same method. Make your money goals line up with your values and change your habits to line up with your goals. And these goals must be relevant and meaningful to the main areas of your life. To become mindful and intentional with your money and get where you want to go in your future, you need to see these connections. Then, you need to set goals relevant to the areas most important to you, and the ones you want to improve to have a well-rounded plan.

The Wheel of Life

You can find plenty of systems and models for dividing the main areas of our lives. None of them are the definitive, be-all-end-all system. However, I've found that author and motivational speaker Zig Ziglar's Wheel of Life presents a clear and comprehensive way to get a pulse on all the essential aspects. This helps you create a healthy balance in all areas of your life. Here are his seven spokes of the wheel:

1. **Mental**. Our thoughts, mindsets, attitudes, behaviors, and mental health.
2. **Spiritual**. Our faith background and/or overall life philosophy or code.
3. **Physical**. Our bodily health and wellness.
4. **Family**. The deep relationships with our kin, especially significant others and children.

5. **Financial**. Our money, which I break down into income, expenses, assets, and debt.
6. **Personal**. Our personal growth and character development. I would also put discipline and consistency in this category. It also covers what we do for fun!
7. **Career**. Our job, especially as it reflects our meaning and purpose in life.

I also like to add an eighth spoke, **Social**. This is our relationships with our friends, acquaintances, and colleagues and what we do for fun.

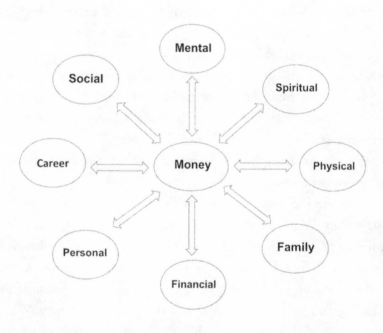

Almost everything we do falls into one or multiple spokes. Money impacts every spoke and every spoke impacts money. And if you take a step back, most if not all of your goals involve one of these spokes, or more than one. Therefore, your financial goals need to take them into account.

It's a two-way street. Let's take a closer look and examine how each spoke influences money, and how money influences each spoke.

Mental Health ⟷ Money

Money and mental health have a reciprocal relationship. Namely, negative feelings translate into spending habits that perpetuate debt. When you're constantly concerned about money and the ability to pay bills, your body reacts with a trauma response.

Poor money habits continue the cycle of negative feelings, making it difficult to improve one without improving the other. High levels of financial stress manifest through physical symptoms like sleep loss, anxiety, headaches/migraines, compromised immune systems, digestive issues, high blood pressure, muscle tension, heart arrhythmia, depression, and a general feeling of being overwhelmed.

It works the other way too, with our mental health affecting our money. When we're not doing well mentally, or have a flawed mindset or attitude, we might hold on to money or make decisions out of fear. We often spend money when we want to feel better. Spending is like dopamine. Dopamine is responsible for allowing you to feel pleasure, satisfaction, and motivation. When you feel good that you have achieved something, it's because you have a surge of dopamine in the brain.

On the flip side, positive mental health will likely attract more money. It allows us to perform better at our job, plus make clearheaded decisions to improve our net worth over time. With a sound mind and surplus emotional energy, we can develop good money habits that serve us deeply. When our money situation thrives, we find ourselves with more peace and calmness.

Spiritual Life ⟷ Money

The term spiritual can mean a variety of things to different people. Some people simply think of it as something beyond themselves, whether that means something spiritual, physical, or a set of ideas like a code or life philosophy. The bottom line is, almost all of us work with or toward a certain meaning and purpose.

For me, I'm a Christian, and this belief significantly impacts my values, priorities, and attitude toward money. Your own life philosophy and religion will affect how you think about money.

While spirituality can impact finances in many ways, not all ways are positive. For example, if you are a Christian like me, some of your beliefs could lead to misconceptions about money. 1 Timothy 6:10 (NIV) reads, "For the love of money is a root of all kinds of evil."

This scripture is often misread that money is the root of all kinds of evil. But if you look closely, you'll see that the *love* of money is the culprit, not money itself. In other words, our attitude toward money matters. We often struggle with greed, wanting more than what we have today to an unnecessary extent. It leads to more stress and pressure in our lives. After all, we're a society of "stuff." We have so much stuff that we have to buy more stuff just to store it all. We've turned our wants into needs.

This leads us to compare what we have to others and feel envy when they seem to have more. We have a drive to "one up" others. Fear of missing out (FOMO) comes up, an emotional response to the thought that someone else is living a better, more satisfying life. This leads us often to feel dissatisfied, stressed, and even depressed. Social media has fueled the fire of comparison by making it so easy to experience comparison. This piles on anxiety and guilt when you feel that you don't measure up to someone else's extravagance. As a result, many people have found themselves in debt by simply trying to keep up with others.

Regardless of your spiritual beliefs and background, being content and satisfied with what you have and where you are is critical. Rather than focusing on what you don't have, focus on what you have. This is an attitude and learned behavior that does not come naturally. When we shift our focus to what we have, we become more grateful and content. Going from greed to contentment is a crucial mindset shift for your journey.

"Whoever loves money never has enough; whoever loves wealth is never satisfied with their income. This too is meaningless." (Ecclesiastes 5:10, NIV)

Principles and Practices for True Profit with Gary Johnson, D. Min

Gary Johnson, D. Min, is the author of *Too Much: Living with Less in the Land of More.* He currently serves as the executive director of e2elders.org, helping elders become effective leaders. On top of this, he has decades of experience teaching biblical principles for personal finance. When asked what he would say to someone curious about what the Bible has to say about money, this is what he said:

I taught as an adjunct professor for many years at seminaries in Lincoln and Cincinnati. One of the classes I would often teach is homiletics [preaching]. I would tell my students that there's a rule of interpreting the Bible: If something is repeated, it's important. If it appears over and over again, God wants to capture our attention. Take, for example, the seven letters to the seven churches in Revelation. Each one ends with, "He who has an ear, let him hear what the Spirit says to the churches." (NKJV)

In the Bible, there are over 2,300 verses about money and the things money can buy. In the Sermon on the Mount, one out of every four verses is about money and the things it can buy. That's 25 percent of the content of Jesus's most famous sermon. Furthermore, nearly one-third of the parables He told are about money.

This means the Word of God is full of wisdom about money and the things it can buy. Why not attempt to become knowledgeable in it and put it into practice? If you do, it will lead to real profit.

When I spoke to Dr. Johnson, he shared four principles, that when added to four daily practices, equal real profit. The winning equation goes like this:

Four Principles + Four Daily Practices = Real Profit

What does he mean by real profit? He means that on top of having a healthier financial outlook, partners will stop arguing about finances. Children will grow up in an environment where their needs are met, and they have an opportunity to learn about personal finance. This kind of peace and harmony is something money can never buy.

The principles Gary shared are these:

1. Contentment. When we accept what we have with a thankful heart, we no longer feel the temptation to live above our means. Living above our means leads to debt.

2. Trust. When we know that God takes care of the flowers of the field and the birds of the air, and promises even more for us, we can navigate financial issues without fear.

3. Gratitude. All things are from God, to God, and for God. A heart of gratitude acknowledges every good gift from Him and leads to contentment, peace, and joy.

4. Humility. Thinking of others as more significant than ourselves will help us have difficult conversations around the topic of money. It will also help us from living beyond our means.

However, beyond just knowing the right principles, Dr. Johnson recommends four daily practices:

1. Giving. When we faithfully bring our tithes and offerings to the Lord, those in need will be supported, and He will bless the work of our hands.

2. Saving. A wise servant takes the deposit from the Lord and brings a return.

3. Budgeting. Jesus explained that one should always count up the cost before they build and steward everything that has been entrusted to them.

4. Living Debt-Free. Proverbs 13:7 states that one person appears rich but is poor, and the other appears poor but is quite wealthy.

Dr. Johnson left me with this thought: "The more we learn this, the stronger our families will be as a result." No matter your faith background, there is wisdom in these principles and daily practices. If you combine them, you will experience real profit.

Physical Health ⟷ Money

Money impacts your physical health in a variety of ways. For instance, it affects the food you buy. Processed, less healthy food is often more affordable for consumers than fresh whole foods; therefore, when shopping on a budget, we often gravitate toward this food choice.

Money also impacts the affordability of personal training, gym memberships, dietitians, nutritionists, and even medical insurance. Plus, stress and anxiety from money will take a toll on your body.

Your physical health impacts your money. When you are physically healthy, you may need to spend less money on medical care. Plus, a physically healthy person will likely have better mental health, indirectly improving their money situation.

Money Conversations and Family with Dustin Sloat

Dustin Sloat is a financial advisor with Edward Jones. He sat down to talk with me about having financial conversations with our children and spouses before sharing four financial habits every family should have. Here's what he had to say:

We develop a money mindset in our early childhood, typically from conversations and things we see modeled by our parents, grandparents, and other older relatives. It's no different with our own children.

How do you feel about discussing money as a parent? According to a recent study, parents are becoming more comfortable about this topic, but there is still some progress to be made. Eighty-six percent of parents surveyed said that they speak with their kids about money. Most of them have a financial conversation at least once per month, with half saying they intentionally talk about money at least twice per month.

An interesting factor that determines whether a parent feels comfortable discussing money with their children comes from the parent's own financial confidence. There's a relationship between feeling confident in your money and feeling confident talking about it with your kids. That's especially important to understand since parents will pass down their money mindset to their children.

So, if you want to get better at talking to your children about money, make sure you take the time to grow your own financial capabilities. And don't worry about having to teach your kids everything at once. When we get better at something, we focus on one aspect at a time. The same goes for money conversations; the aspect you discuss will depend on the child's age and stage, as well as relevant topics to your household. This could mean you talk about what it means to save their allowance, all the way to saving for a house.

Additionally, make sure you and your partner (or potential partner) are on the same page as you age and get into big earning and saving years. Make a list of your accounts, investments, and debts. Consider your wants versus your needs and map them out. Make sure you know where important legal documents can be found. Finally, consider

*end-of-life planning. I know these can be intim-
idating topics, but it's vital to talk through them
with someone who will share your life and finances
with you.*

*Lastly, start small. You don't need to change all of
your family's financial habits overnight. Begin by
writing down your needs and wants. Decide how
you will navigate borrowing and debt. Build emergency savings. Talk through big financial decisions
with your family, and bring children into these
conversations so they see how you process them.
If you slowly but surely create these habits, you'll
be on your way to a stronger financial picture and
more confident kids.*

Note: The author of this book and Dustin Sloat have an
existing business relationship. This information is not a
testimonial of the services provided by Edward Jones.

Family ⟷ Money

Money has a profound effect on your family. It is one of the
biggest reasons for divorce and family conflict. You instill money
values into your children, just like your family of origin did for
you.

Your family affects your money. Families have different habits,
attitudes, and values when it comes to money. You and I have
developed money scripts, habits, attitudes, and values stemming

from our parents and other family members, some of which we're not even aware of.

Financial Health ⟷ Money

It's a no-brainer that money impacts financial health, but financial health means much more than just money. It is the state and stability of an individual's personal finances that includes spending, saving, borrowing, and planning in ways that will enable them to be resilient and pursue opportunities. The Consumer Financial Protection Bureau talked to consumers and experts from all over the nation and discovered four elements of financial health:[3]

1. Feeling in control
2. Capacity to absorb a financial shock
3. On track to meet goals
4. Flexibility to make choices

Personal ⟷ Money

Money helps you afford hobbies and gives you the means to purchase any products that help you grow personally. This includes things such as buying books, taking courses, paying for college tuition, and attending conferences. Improving your skills and character typically requires money in some form; even "free" resources online require a cell phone or computer and an internet connection, or transportation to a public library.

Personal growth in terms of discipline and consistency will help you more than anything else on your journey toward your

---

3   Consumer Financial Protection Bureau, "Financial Well-Being: The Goal of Financial Education," ConsumerFinance.gov, January 2015, https://files. consumerfinance.gov/f/201501_cfpb_report_financial-well-being.pdf.

financial goals. Getting to your vision requires clear goals and habits to power you at every step of the journey.

Career ⟷ Money

Money greatly influences your career, and of course, your career influences your money. People with more money could gain the freedom to walk away from a high-paying job they don't like into something that pays less but aligns with their passions. Money also helps you afford training for skills and networking events to advance in your career.

Growing in your career will raise your income and give you access to certain kinds of assets, such as retirement and investment plans. The way you manage money will change depending on whether you work as a contractor, an employee, or a business owner. Each of those will come with its own advantages and disadvantages for your financial picture.

Social Life ⟷ Money

Your relationships have a large impact on your money. Do spendy friends frequently pressure you to go out or take a trip? Do neighbors brag about big purchases? Do nosy family members always have an opinion about your financial habits? To preserve a healthy relationship with your money, you may have to set boundaries with certain social circles.

The people you surround yourself with matter. It's beneficial to remain close to those who generally share the same financial outlook as you. People who have good relationships with their money will influence you to keep a good relationship too. Focus on how they help you rather than making comparisons. That's not to say you can't be friends with those who have poor financial habits. You must be mindful and make sure this friendship does not create chaos in your finances.

It's a Domino Effect

We've talked about the interplay between money and the eight main areas of life. It may seem overwhelming to think about goals to improve in every area. That's why I love sharing this fact: Improving in one aspect tends to lead to improvements in other aspects. In other words, you don't have to burn yourself out working to fix eight areas in your life to have a good financial situation. Additionally, focusing on setting and achieving your financial goals will lead to improvements in all those areas as a natural byproduct.

Here's what I'm talking about: When a person gets their finances in order, begins making more money, and has a higher net worth, it tends to improve their mental health. They worry less and they sleep better. It gives them a better outlook on the future.

Having good mental health will help with your social life and family relationships. Because families and couples tend to fight over money, removing money stress from the equation gives you more relational harmony. Plus, you can afford to have a more robust social life if you aren't worried about spending money on things you enjoy, such as concert tickets or eating at a restaurant.

If you have a harmonious family life and a strong social network, it will lead to better career opportunities for you. That's the reason for the popular adage "Show me your network, and I'll show you your net worth," popularized by author Porter Gale. The right friend could lead you to the perfect job.

A better job improves your overall financial picture. This further solidifies your financial situation, potentially giving you the income and benefits to improve and maintain your physical fitness and health. Plus, you'll likely have money left over for spiritual practices, charitable giving, and personal growth.

It's a lovely domino effect once you get started. Now, I'm not saying that the steps outlined above are the only path, but merely an example. I'm telling you not to be surprised when you get your finances in order and then suddenly find other areas of your life improving too. That's one of the greatest joys about what I do. As I help people become more mindful and intentional about their money, I see a positive life change.

Now What?

Now that we've gone over the eight areas, how money affects them (and vice versa), and given examples of how they all work together, it's time to incorporate that information into our plan.

[Use the Companion Guide to rank yourself in each area of life.]

A 10 means you are thriving and cannot possibly think of any improvements to make. A 1 means that it's terrible, and it's hard to see how things could ever improve. Be completely honest with yourself. This is a judgment- and guilt-free zone. Here they are again:

- Mental
- Spiritual
- Physical
- Family
- Financial
- Personal
- Career
- Social

Take your time and think deeply about each one as you go. Most people will have a few areas that are doing well, some that are doing fine, and one or two that need some attention. It's totally okay if you think you're doing better or worse than average. Don't compare yourself to where others are, or where society thinks you need to be.

After you rank them, decide one or two you want to focus on. Your money goals should be directly related to these areas. As you reach your financial vision, you'll find these aspects dramatically improving.

Eventually, you should have a goal for every area of your life. Balance is the key. Because every aspect of your life impacts the other aspects (as we talked about above), you'll find significant overlap between them. Plus, you'll find money has a huge influence on each one.

After this, it's time to set goals.

Strategize

Remember the example of the treadmill? That's what it's like to have a general desire to improve in areas of your life, but never set goals or make a plan. If you don't set goals and make deliberate changes, you will most likely stay in the same place. In five years, you'll be where you are now. Is that what you want?

Again, I'm not trying to impose values on you. This is about what you want for yourself, achieving your vision for the future. It's up to you to create the future you desire. I'm telling you that the best way to do that is through setting well-established goals (reached by employing the right habits), aligning with your values, and targeting the areas of life you prioritize the most. See how it all ties together?

All the information we've covered so far helps us to see our financial snapshot and how it affects our life; it shows us the areas we may want to focus on for our goals.

Money as a Tool for Your "Buckets" with Teresa McCloy

Teresa McCloy is the founder and creator of the REAL-IFE Process. She coaches leaders, speakers, and trainers on how to develop and diversify their businesses and nonprofits. Her team provides both certification and coaching, helping organizations increase their impact on the world and create revenue from that impact.

When Teresa begins working with someone personally, she learns about the "buckets" in their life. According to Teresa, everyone has five to seven areas in their life that matter most to them, which constitute their buckets. Sound familiar? Plus, there's one thing that all of her clients tell her is a priority bucket: Finances.

Some of them come at it from the angle of wealth. Others from the angle of generosity, or wealth building. It depends on their season of life. But the bottom line is, according to Teresa, "Everyone has money as part of their story because we all have a story about money."

This story about money impacts our money behavior. There's a tape you play in your head about money. Teresa and her team help people rewrite those scripts into something new and believable, an area of focus. Instead of letting money dictate their lifestyle, relationships, mental and physical health, work, and so on, she teaches them how to navigate with it.

In Teresa's own career, she has been an entrepreneur all her life. She remembers selling Christmas cards door to door when she was less than ten years old. Her script became "I want my own money, money I can control. This will bring me freedom." This caused her to work more, and work harder, and always try new ideas for making money. When she got married, she still worked several different jobs. She wanted to have her own money and spending money because money gave her the freedom she wanted.

This led to Teresa starting a brick-and-mortar retail business before the internet and e-commerce. She knew how to work hard, but she didn't know how to manage the backend of this kind of business. Her business began to lose money, and in a moment of desperation, she borrowed money without telling her husband.

When the business still went under, she remembers the difficult conversation of having to share what she had done with her husband and the ten-year-long process of paying everything back. This led her to flip the script in her own life.

Instead of treating money as the be-all-end-all, she began to treat money as a tool to get her to her goals. She learned that she didn't need to earn a ton of money to feel in control but began finding more satisfaction from her relationships and work. This led her to take all the lessons she had learned and begin her successful consulting business.

When she started her current business, she felt the doubts in the back of her mind from her previous failed business. Would she be successful and handle it well? "Our stories never completely go away. We can reshape and reform them, though," Teresa shared. Ultimately, she told herself a new story about money and used it as a tool to help her in all of her own buckets.

Next up, we'll cover how to set goals we can actually achieve by doing it SMARTER.

Chapter Summary

Walking through our financial life—and life in general—without goals is like running on a treadmill. We are working hard, but not going anywhere. We need the right goals to move forward. What are the right goals? They're goals that target the areas of our life most important to us, set with an understanding of how money influences those areas. When we understand the wheel of life and how each spoke influences each other, we can begin to build the kind of future we want through our goals.

KEY TAKEAWAYS

- The Wheel of Life contains eight components that impact money: Mental, Spiritual, Physical, Financial, Family, Personal, Career, and Social.
- You have determined which areas of your life are thriving and which areas need improvement. Consider changes that could be made in areas that need improvement.
- Make the decision to get off the treadmill and start walking toward your vision.

CHAPTER 3:

Setting SMARTER Goals

Go to work, get paid, and pay your bills. Go to work, get paid, and pay your bills. Go to work, get paid, and pay your bills. You get the idea; it's a vicious cycle. After a while, you will think, *Is there more to life than this?* If you don't make changes, my guess is the answer is "No!" Or you might ask, "Will I still be doing this same thing thirty or forty years from now?" If you don't make changes, my guess is the answer is "Yes!" If you don't change your thinking and behavior, I pretty much guarantee this will be your future. This might be fine if you're content. If not, start thinking now about where you want to be in five, ten, or fifteen years.

How many years, around January 1, have we said to ourselves, "This is it; this is the year that I'm going to do this. I'm going to achieve all my New Year's resolutions!" You're excited, motivated, and pumped to make this happen . . . for about one week. Then you start sliding into old habits and lose focus on those resolutions you committed to just one week ago. The thing is, they are usually the same resolutions that you have been making for the past ten years! Come February 1, you're thinking, *What resolutions?*

We've been doing it all wrong for years in how we set and think about our goals. It's all in how you approach, think about, and develop goal-setting strategies that determine whether you will reach them.

We need to shift to set our goals mindfully and intentionally. This allows us to set goals in a fashion that makes us see progress and not give up. The approach you take in how you think about your goals will determine whether you will reach them.

Do you achieve your New Year's resolutions? If so, congratulations and keep it up. Even so, you will most likely find something new in this chapter to refine your goal-setting process. However, if you're like most people who have trouble sticking to their goals, I have good news for you. You're about to learn a system that will increase the odds of achieving them.

We're going to learn a foundational goal-setting process, learn how to work in the "why" that we discussed in the past couple of chapters, make a simple-to-follow plan, and focus on the areas that matter most. Failure to do any of these is why most people don't make it. It's all about the process.

Why Set Goals?

Goal setting ought to be one of the first steps in making a financial plan. Your goals give you a road map to stay on course. Without them, you can't progress from where you are now to where you want to be. You might not be where you want to go yet, but having the assurance that you're moving in the right direction? That's priceless. Additionally, you'll be even more motivated than before because you know your goals line up with your values and beliefs and target the specific life circumstances you want to improve. Once established, your habits will follow.

Goals require you to create and sustain a lifetime change. Remember when we talked about how improving in one aspect of your life tends to improve the other ones? This is how. It's the fuel needed to create positive change across the board. That's also why goals are hard. If your goal doesn't require change, it isn't significant. It won't matter whether you achieve it or not. You will not become a new kind of person, one capable of sustaining growth in your income and net worth.

If you don't set goals, you will continue to mindlessly spend and save money with no purpose or future direction. Having a plan and visualizing your outcomes, rather than simply shifting money around, will help you gain control and give you a purpose. Keeping track of your progress and reaching milestones encourages you to keep pushing forward. Mindful spending and goal setting go hand in hand, helping you stay in line with your stated values and beliefs. Overall, the process leads to more contentment, and you will see your vision slowly coming to life.

Basic Rules

This goal-setting system is called SMARTER goals, closely related to another system you may have heard of called SMART goals. SMARTER goals add a couple of extra elements to the process that will make you feel more motivated and stay on track. Before I explain the SMARTER system, let me give a few insights.

1. **Set reasonably high goals.** Your goals should be set high, but not too high. They should be challenging enough that it requires a change in your habits and lifestyle to achieve them. This way, when you reach a goal, it will mean something. On the other end of the spectrum, they shouldn't

be impossible to achieve because that will leave you feeling discouraged.

2. **Don't set your goals in concrete.** Throughout this process, you may set long-term goals that will take years to achieve. Don't hold on to them with a white-knuckle grip. As your life stage changes, you might find your goals adapting with the times or situations beyond your control may prevent you from staying on this path. Does this mean you set no long-term goals since they might change? No. It simply means you reevaluate your goals periodically to make sure they're still what you want, and in between evaluations, you keep working hard toward them.

3. **Place your goals where you can review them daily.** This is one of the best ways to ensure you reach your goals. Out of sight means out of mind. What we look at becomes what we pay attention to and focus on. Make sure you remind yourself of your goals every day. You could make them your phone's lock screen background or put them on a sticky note in your bathroom mirror. Do whatever it takes to remind yourself of your goals each day. Also, know that some days may come along when you feel unmotivated and just want to "be" rather than thinking about and positioning for your future. That's fine. Don't feel guilty about those days.

Setting SMARTER Goals

In my opinion, these goals are the most optimal strategy for mindful and intentional money. Each aspect of SMARTER goals is covered by one of the letters in the word so you can remember them. Here are the criteria:

S for Specific: Be as specific as possible with what you want to accomplish. Instead of saying "I want to save more money," say something like "I want to begin saving $200 each month in a retirement savings account." The more clear and precise, the better. Additionally, set the goal positively instead of negatively. Don't say "I will stop using my credit card," but say "I will make every purchase with cash or debit."

Being specific also helps you break the goal down into smaller chunks to mark your progress. Focus on your progress and effort instead of the outcome. Instead of saying "I will invest $30,000 into my retirement over the next five years," say "I will invest $6,000 each year," or even better, "$500 each month."

M for Measurable: If you don't have a way to measure your goal, you will not know whether you've reached it. In terms of financial goals, this typically looks like putting specific dollar amounts on each goal. Which is better, saying "I want to save more money," or saying "I want to save up $10,000"? The one you can measure, of course!

A for Achievable: When you set your goals, make sure you have the skill set and tools necessary to accomplish them. This goes back to the idea of not setting impossibly high goals. Does your goal match your current abilities and financial situation? Is there anything you'll need to learn in order to reach the goal? This is also where you start thinking about who else will need to be involved so you can reach this goal. This could mean bringing your significant other into the goal-setting process or reaching out to find a financial coach or advisor.

R for Relevant: This goes back to the why. The goal you set should be relevant to one or more of the eight areas of life we discussed in the last chapter. This provides a sense of motivation to accomplish the goal, and it ensures that a specific area of your life will improve when you reach the goal. In other words, it makes the process more rewarding. Take the time to determine the personal significance of this goal.

T for Time-Bound: A goal without a deadline is more like a dream or a wish. Making the goal time-bound gives you a reason to move toward it each day. To this end, set a deadline for the goal that is relatively challenging, but possible to accomplish. For example, you may not be able to save up for a down payment on a house this month, but it could be something you accomplish within twelve to twenty-four months.

These are the criteria for SMART goals, but let's take it a couple of steps further. Instead of having SMART goals, we set SMARTER goals. This adds the following two criteria:

E for Exciting: Take the time to visualize the outcome. Does it make you feel excited? Does it markedly improve your life in some aspect? If the thought of achieving this goal doesn't make you feel energized and fired up to get started, consider thinking bigger or targeting a different area. This emotional fuel is necessary to make the first few changes and solidify your financial habits.

R for Recorded: What good is a SMART goal if you don't write it down or remind yourself of it? This goes back to our rule about putting our goals where we can see them every day. If you write down your goals instead of just thinking about them mentally, you'll remember them better for one, and for two, you'll be able to accurately measure your progress toward them.

[Use the Companion Guide to set your SMARTER goals.]

If You Fail to Plan, You Plan to Fail

This planning process might feel overwhelming at first. Just know that over time, as you push through the initial avoidance, it will reduce your overall stress. This process gives you priorities, which helps you develop a simple action plan and makes your progress habitual. It will begin to happen naturally instead of becoming something you need to think or worry about.

Some goals will be much easier to achieve than others, like a goal to get out of short-term debt as opposed to a goal to pay off a house. The quick goals will give you the confidence and motivation to keep moving toward the goals that take more time and discipline. That's why we should categorize our goals into short, intermediate, and long term.

Short-Term Goals take a year or less to achieve. They are foundational goals that make it easier to reach the bigger goals. Here are some examples of short-term goals:

- Become a mindful and intentional spender. Take a month to keep track of all the money you spend, how you feel while spending it, and the area of life this purchase impacts. Simply keeping track of what you spend will likely help you see a few surprising patterns. I hope that you set this as one of your goals!

- Make a budget. A budget is nothing more than a spending plan that takes into account your income and expenses. It is the foundation of mindful money. If you don't have a budget yet, this should be a priority.

- Pay off the credit card. Get rid of debt, as it will hold you back from long-term savings and investments.

- Create an emergency fund. This is a must-have; a savings account you would use in the case that you had a sudden unexpected expense. Or you would use it if you lost a job unexpectedly. These funds should cover three to six months' worth of expenses.

My youngest daughter moved away to the East Coast. At one point, I suggested to her the importance of having an emergency fund for unexpected expenses that might come up such as a flat tire, car repair, etc. With a sarcastic tone and an eye roll, she responded with, "I'm not going to have an emergency." She stopped just short of saying, "Mom, you are so dumb." Put simply, she did not feel the need for this fund. I said my piece and let it go but reminded her that the "bank of mom and dad" is closed.

A couple of months later, a severe hurricane hit the East Coast. This required that she and ten of her friends relocate inland to a Vrbo for ten days. She did not receive a paycheck during that time period. This was my teachable moment, reiterating the importance of having an emergency fund for situations such as this. It often takes difficult life experiences to learn money lessons. Let's just say that she now has an emergency fund in place.

Intermediate Goals take a bit longer, maybe two or three years to reach. They fall in between the long term and short term. Perhaps after achieving some short-term goals, you'll have the confidence to shoot for something bigger and more impactful to your life. Examples include the following:

- Paying down (or off) student loans. Your debt will decrease much more quickly if you pay more than your minimum payment each month. When the loans are paid off, it will increase your net income each month by a large margin— and will feel amazing.
- Saving up for a vacation or wedding. People know that vacations and weddings are coming, but not everyone

saves up for them early enough. Then, they charge many of the expenses to their credit card and end up in debt. Take the date of the wedding or vacation, work backward, and calculate how much you need to save each month to get there.

- Purchasing a vehicle. Make the largest down payment possible, or even better, pay off the vehicle in full. Then, if you have a loan, make it the shortest term possible to reduce the amount of interest you will pay. Think about it, having an emergency fund, no credit card debt, and a paid-off vehicle will help your mental health too.

Long-Term Goals generally take five-plus years to accomplish. They also have the highest degree of satisfaction attached to them. Long-term goal examples include the following:

- Buying or paying off a home. Depending on your life stage, this could be an intermediate goal. However, for many people, it's one of the most significant purchases of a lifetime. Having a fully paid-off house is a dream, and I can tell you from experience, it feels awesome! If you don't have one yet, a good long-term goal could be to save the largest possible down payment to lower your mortgage payments, and then to pay even more than your minimum payment each month to reduce the loan principal quicker.
- Saving for retirement. My motto is "Play now, pay later, or pay now, play later." If you spend extraordinary amounts of money now, you'll have far less for retirement and will be working into your retirement years rather than playing. If you pay now, you'll be able to play exponentially more later because of the power of compounding interest.

Break down all your goals, especially the long-term ones, into shorter time frames that you can measure and track. Instead of thinking about paying off your home, think about how much you can pay off this year. I recommend setting a goal in each category that targets the areas of life that we discussed in chapter 2. Focus on the ones that you're most passionate about right now.

Start by setting one long-term financial goal. This could mean a down payment for a house, paying off student loans, saving for a vacation or retirement, or building an emergency fund. These are just suggestions; you might have something else in mind.

Now, you can begin working toward this future with your present action. This is done by breaking down the long-term goals into smaller goals with a much shorter time period. For example, if your goal will take ten years to accomplish, you should break it down into subgoals of five years, and then break those down into one- to two-year goals. This will help you stay motivated seeing the accomplishments when reaching the shorter-term goals.

[Use your Companion Guide to create and record your SMARTER goals.]

Breaking It Down

Goal setting requires you to change your habits. It isn't a "quick fix" kind of thing. When you have your long-term goal established, you can use it to set intermediate subgoals as a halfway point to your main goal. It might mean setting up multiple intermediate goals, like steps on a ladder until you get to the place you want to be.

[In your Companion Guide, develop that first long-term goal.]

Make sure your goal is measurable and has a deadline. Make sure the prospect of achieving it within the time frame feels exciting to you. Lastly, make sure it's relevant to the areas of life you want to improve.

Once you write down your long-term goal, write out two to five intermediate goals that will help you get there. Then, for each intermediate goal, write down short-term goals that help you accomplish them.

This all gives you an idea of what you need to do each day, week, and month. When you hit your short-term goals, you know you're on track for your intermediate goals. This gives you confidence that your long-term goals are getting closer too. It's important to connect the relevance of what you do today with the destination you want to reach in five, ten, or even thirty years.

Because of that, you should write out a list of what you need to do each day, week, or month to achieve your vision.

[Again, use your Companion Guide to map out your task list.]

Get Motivated

Well done! You've identified a long-term goal and broken it down into smaller steps. This will give you immense motivation as you check off smaller items that lead to bigger ones. Now, follow these steps to get yourself motivated and stay in that space over the long term:

1. Review your goals daily. Place them on your phone, on the bathroom mirror, on your refrigerator, or by your bedside. Perhaps it will be a picture of your dream home taped to the front door you walk through each morning. If you're visually minded, you can make a collage with images of your goals that not only looks good but fuels your achievement.

2. Review your progress often. Schedule a daily, weekly, and/ or monthly check-in with yourself. Analyze your progress. Did you perform the tasks you needed to? Did your

efforts lead to a short-term goal being accomplished? If not, adjust your efforts.

3. Establish a reward system for yourself. How will you celebrate when you reach a goal? It could look like time spent doing something you love or a favorite food. Celebrate the small victories to motivate you to stay on track.

4. Don't stress if you get off track. You're human. This means you're bound to fall off the wagon at some point. Allow yourself a "vacation" day to step away and just "be"—not worrying or thinking about your future. When a setback happens, don't catastrophize, or treat it like all your progress was for nothing. You can and will do better next time. Remain flexible, as life seems to have a way of delaying our timeline and making us revise our plans. It's okay when your goals evolve over time.

5. Focus on today. You can't control one week from now, far less a month, a year, or ten years. But you know that what you do today directly corresponds to your vision. So, if you do what you need to do today, you will have won. Nobody can take that away from you. This will turn every evening into a celebration as you get 1 percent closer to the finish line.

6. Share your goals with the right people. This will keep you accountable and working toward your goals. When you know that someone else knows about your goal, you'll feel more motivated. However, make sure that person will be positive and serve as a support system. If someone brings you down or expresses doubt or discouragement, don't share your goals with them.

7. Set individual and family/household goals. If you have a spouse or significant other, you should team up for some

long-term goals. Make sure you are riding on the same train and going in the same direction. This may require compromise, but it is far better than a tug-of-war heading in opposite directions. However, you can each set goals that line up with your personal desires separately. That way, you get the best of both worlds.

We covered where money habits, attitudes, and values come from. We talked about the most important areas of life and how money impacts them. Then, we learned how to set goals that line up with our values and vision. This effectively gives us our vision for the future. In the following section, we'll learn how to create a crystal-clear snapshot of our current financial situation. We can't get where we want to go without knowing where we are.

Remember, we need to know where we're going, where we are, then learn, plan, and execute. Next, we'll talk about knowing where you are.

Chapter Summary

SMARTER goals go beyond SMART goals. They are specific, measurable, achievable, relevant, and time-bound, which are all fantastic attributes. They also add excitement and are recorded to give an extra boost to their attainability. By putting that goal in front of you every day, reviewing and celebrating progress, and developing a support system, you have a much higher chance of achieving your goals than, say, a New Year's resolution.

KEY TAKEAWAYS

- Developing a solid, strategic plan is necessary to successfully reach your goals.
- Using the SMARTER system, long-term goals must be broken down into intermediate and short-term goals to be successful. These goals will influence your daily, weekly, and monthly actions.
- Get into the habit of celebrating yourself when you make progress. You've already come further than many people do, and you're taking control of your financial picture from here on out.
- Additional tables and more resources are available in the Companion Guide.

ANCHORD MONEY

Part 2:

KNOW WHERE YOU ARE

When you start a puzzle, you dump the pieces out of the box and essentially have chaos. So you need to put those pieces together. Because of the picture on the box, you have the image in mind, but you don't yet know how everything fits together. The same is true in your financial picture.

To get started, we must understand where we are today. That's our snapshot. So far, we've talked about how we got where we are through our money scripts, personality, habits, attitudes, and values. We also looked at how money impacts every area of our lives and how to set goals in alignment with this. To sum up, we have our destination and road map.

But where are we today? That's where the snapshot comes in. Now that all the pieces are out of the box, we need to identify, sort, and organize them, so they will fit together. This is your starting point when you first tackle this puzzle.

In terms of a financial snapshot, you may find yourself with a high income—but scattered pieces elsewhere, like in your debt and mindless spending. If you have high amounts of debt and your expenses nearly or completely outpace your income, that negates your high earnings. Think about it, I'm sure you have worked hard for that high income, so you want that to work in your favor financially. Or perhaps you have lower income but no debt, and thus positive net worth. Now, you're wanting to put your income to work to have a more comfortable, secure future.

Now we want to look at the pieces of your financial puzzle. We'll strategically and methodically put the pieces together—turn the chaos into calm. What are the puzzle pieces? They are your income, expenses, assets, debt, and net worth. Each piece fits predominantly into one or two other pieces, coming together into a holistic picture. The next chapters will dive deep into definitions for each and how to measure and track them.

What is the final picture, the goal? For most people, it's increasing net worth. Your net worth is your true wealth, as opposed to income. For example, someone with a net worth of $1 million and increasing is better off than someone with $1 million in income but millions in debt. We often get caught up in the idea that "I need to make more money in order to be wealthy." That's a misconception.

The truth is more like, "I need my income and assets to be bigger than my expenses and debt, respectively, and continue trending in that direction." Or, put more simply, "I need my net worth to increase in order to be wealthy." When you increase income and assets and reduce your expenses and debt, your net worth will increase, thus improving your overall financial situation.

Understanding where you are now and where you need to be will set you up for success in this area. You need to create a plan and execute it to get from the snapshot of today to the vision of tomorrow.

One final note: Reserve self-judgment and comparison, that's not what we're about. You may feel guilty or ashamed of your spending habits or debt. You might be tempted to compare yourself with someone who's making more or appears to have higher net worth. That's not what we're about. No matter what your snapshot looks like, you can follow the plan to get to *your* vision. It starts with understanding the puzzle pieces.

Breaking down your snapshot into five sections—namely, Your Income, Your Expenses, Your Assets, Your Debt, and Your Net Worth—will illustrate your current financial situation.

CHAPTER 4:

Your Income

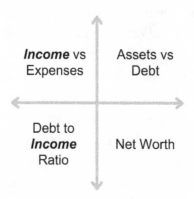

Income vs Expenses	Assets vs Debt
Debt to *Income* Ratio	Net Worth

here are four primary measures of your financial snapshot:
1. **Income** vs. Expenses
2. Assets vs. Debt
3. Debt-to-**Income** (DTI) Ratio
4. Net Worth

We'll cover what these are, how to calculate them, and what to do with them in this section. This will give you a financial snapshot to work with.

Here's another financial scenario that happened with my East Coast daughter. When she first moved there, she made good money working in the service industry. Tourists gave her good tips. After a few years, though, she knew this wasn't her destiny. She wanted to get what she called a "big girl" job. This led to her landing a wonderful job in a great environment . . . but with a pay cut. This new job didn't have tips.

As we prepared a trip to visit her, she said the magic words: "Mom, I need help with my finances." All excited, I packed up my course materials and off we went for an opportunity for intentional financial instruction!

My first task for her was to complete the expenditure sheet. She wrote down all her expenses for one month (I didn't look at this sheet since I knew it would provoke unwelcome advice). Then, I asked her to write down her total income for a month. She handed me both sums and I reviewed them.

I saw the numbers, handed the papers back, and said, "You either need to get a second job or stop spending so much money. You can't make ends meet with what you're earning." Oh boy, that did not go over well. With that same sarcastic tone and eye roll as the emergency fund lesson, and this time, some shoulder action, she said, "Just when am I supposed to work a second job? I work eight to four thirty, Monday through Friday." I told her that there's always evenings and weekends! Her dad and I often worked two or three jobs each over the years when we had to. It isn't forever, but sometimes it's necessary. A second job can hold you over until you get a raise, bonus, or promotion.

My daughter was confident that her expenses were as low as they could be. So she decided to pick up a second job in the service sector to get the tips rolling in again. After about six months, she was able to make ends meet with her one job.

Here's a similar scenario that underlines how income fits into our financial snapshot:

Picture two individuals named Beth and Dante. Both Beth and Dante make $100,000 each year from their jobs. That's a decent accomplishment in and of itself, and it should give them both a solid financial snapshot, right? Not necessarily. Income is just one piece of the puzzle. Its relationship to the other pieces of the puzzle, especially expenses, can be the difference between chaos and calm.

In the last year, Dante spent all his money and then some, ending up $10,000 in credit card debt. On the other hand, Beth spent $50,000 of her income and invested the rest. Which of these two has the healthiest financial snapshot?

Definitely the one who spends less money than they make.

Imagine instead that Dante makes $200,000 per year, and Beth still makes $100,000. In this example, Dante spends all that money. Beth still has a healthier financial snapshot because she has an extra $50,000 to work with each year, and Dante has nothing. Beth can move toward a higher net worth than Dante over time. Even though Dante has double the income, he's in financial trouble.

Now, if Dante got his financial habits corrected, and set goals that align with his values and attitudes, he would be able to grow his net worth faster. After all, he has twice as much money coming in, so that gives him more to invest to increase his net worth.

Currently, he's not in the healthiest situation. The one who spends less will feel like their income is helping them more, even if they have less of it. That's a crucial thing to remember when talking about income because many people create a false equivalence between "income" and "wealth." Income is one piece of the puzzle, but it must be examined in relation to the other parts.

So the income you make is important, but not as important as your **income vs. expenses**.

This chapter discusses income, the first half of the income to expenses calculation. The next four chapters will cover expenses, assets, debts, and net worth to complete your financial picture.

First, is learning how to calculate income vs. expenses. Don't cringe at the word "calculate." You may have purchased this book because you don't like math, and I promised you don't have to be a math wizard. You still don't. Every calculation will be made as simple as possible

For now, it's vital to remember that income doesn't exist in a silo. In other words, making a ton of money doesn't mean you have a good financial snapshot. Just ask Dante.

Income: The First Half of Your Income vs. Expenses

To calculate income vs. expenses, simply subtract expenses from income. This will give you a positive or a negative number, which represents a surplus or a deficit. To derive your income, take a step back and consider all its sources.

When you think of income, you often think of wages and salary; however, income goes beyond just what you do for a job. It doesn't end with your monthly or biweekly paycheck. Instead, it's *all* the money you have coming in. Here is a brief list of other ways you could increase your income besides your primary job:

- Bonuses
- Selling stuff and decluttering your home
- Trading securities
- Receiving monetary gifts
- Side hustles
- Dividends from investments
- Retirement plans and pensions
- Social security

If you look at all the money that came to you over the last year, you might see these types of income. Perhaps you got a bonus from your workplace around Christmas, or you received a monetary birthday gift.

So, instead of thinking about income solely as your regular wages and salary, think of it more broadly. Your income is the money that is brought in throughout the year.

I find this definition more helpful because it gives us more control and freedom. It can be difficult to control how much you get paid at your job. It takes time to learn new skills, accrue experience, and get promoted. However, you can increase your income apart from your regular job—and it's easier than you think. Here's an example:

You probably have at least $2,000 worth of used items in your house. This is the "stuff," the clutter that accumulates as life goes on; some of it in the form of furniture that no one sits on. It could also be electronics sitting in a drawer, gathering dust. Maybe it's exercise equipment, that if we're being honest, we never use.

If you had a sudden, unexpected bill for $2,000 that you had to pay, you could probably find that money between the four walls of your home, in the form of stuff. Some of us even have items in a storage container that has a monthly fee, or items lying around in our (or our parents') garage.

You could go on an online marketplace and see similar items to your own listed. There's no reason you couldn't sell this stuff if you had to. After all, there's nothing stopping you from selling your sectional and then buying an even better one later once your financial situation has improved. These aren't priceless heirlooms, but the stuff that adds up over time.

A few years back, I decided to purge stuff around our house. If I looked at something and didn't say "wow," out the door it went.

As I mentioned earlier, our philosophy now is to consider whether our kids will want it rather than whether we want it.

So, if I'm coaching someone on their finances, that's one of the first things I look at. A person can immediately boost their income vs. expenses by emptying out a storage unit, selling everything they can, and canceling their storage unit rent. Not only would that lower their monthly expenses, but it would give them a small boost in income that they could use to pay off or put toward credit card debt or invest.

The truth is, we often have more than we need. And almost anything we part with, we can buy back later when our financial situation improves. This applies to most objects in your home, except that which has irreplaceable sentimental value.

The bottom line is, begin thinking of income as all the money coming in, not just your paychecks. This will give you freedom and enable you to think about opportunities to increase your income.

Calculating Your Income

To calculate your income vs. expenses, you need to know your total income.

For this number, I would recommend coming up with your expected monthly income. It should be your net income instead of your gross income; in other words, the amount of money you've earned after taxes. This is the actual amount of money you receive in your paycheck if you have a typical W-2 job. Other sources of income will be added, so the process ends up looking like this:

1. Review Your Paychecks

Get the amount of pay you received after taxes. If you have irregular pay, or you're a sole proprietor or business owner, it can be difficult to calculate this. In this instance, I recommend taking a low-performing month and using that number. That way, making more than that figure feels like a bonus. Remember, don't count the income you withhold for tax payments.

2. Add Your Side Hustle Income
Some people work multiple jobs, or moonlight in the gig economy such as driving people around, shopping for groceries, or doing freelance work in the evenings. Make sure to add what you can expect in a month from these hustles. Again, add the amount after taxes.

3. Include Sales of Securities and Assets
Not everyone has money in the stock market or invested in real estate, but if you do, you should include it here. This could look like money made day trading, rent coming from renters, or the sale of land.

4. Sell Stuff
Don't forget that the stuff around your house counts as assets. You could commit to selling $200–$500 worth of stuff each month, and count that as part of your income.

5. Add Any Dividends, Pensions, Social Security, etc.
Some people have regular payouts through dividends from a trust, a pension from their career, social security, an insurance payout, you name it. Don't forget to include these.

6. Predict Miscellaneous Income
This includes monetary gifts and bonuses. At the end of this calculation, it could be helpful to go over your bank balance from the last couple of months and see whether any income has come in

that doesn't match the categories above. You can use this to predict how much you'll get from these sources, on average, each month.

[Use the chart in your Companion Guide to calculate your total income.]

After following these steps, you'll have a good idea of what you can expect to make in the average month. Notice how it takes into account income from all sources, and not just your regular pay. This gives you the power to increase your income if you need to.

When someone begins learning from me, they usually have some idea of their financial snapshot. They might have high debt, out-of-control expenses, or feel like they're heading in the wrong direction in their net worth. One of the first strategies I recommend is paying off debt to improve your income vs. expenses picture. To do this, it often requires temporarily increasing your income, reducing monthly expenses, or a combination of both.

The more money coming in, the quicker you can move toward a place of positive and growing net worth. Along with reducing expenses, it's a fantastic first step. Chapter 11 provides more detailed opportunities to increase income after we go over the other numbers we need for our financial snapshot.

Becoming Mindful and Intentional with Income

Income is a significant piece of the puzzle and is the foundation of your financial snapshot. That's why it was the first step. Next up, is how to calculate your expenses, then how to subtract expenses from your income, and finally, how to improve that surplus/deficit. That will give you one of the three major pieces that you will use to measure your financial snapshot, and more ideas about how to improve it in the short and long term.

The key here is becoming more mindful and intentional with your income. As you've repeatedly been told, everyone has different money scripts, personalities, habits, attitudes, and values regarding money. This sets the stage for the way you think about your income. When people come to me, they tend to view money in terms of scarcity, thinking about how all their income is about to go away into expenses and debt. Or they think of money in terms of overabundance, and when payday comes, they think about all the fun things to spend their money on without regard to their expenses.

Instead, think of income as a tool. Nothing more, nothing less. It's a lever you pull to boost your net worth, in relation to the other levers. I find this analogy takes some emotion and worry out of the equation.

Plus, when you get mindful with your income, you begin to discover more opportunities. Many people I work with feel stuck in terms of income because they have a fixed income and a fixed mindset. They can't see beyond their paycheck on the tenth and twenty-fifth of each month and think of new opportunities. Through this process, they begin to see that they can increase their income in a variety of ways and take control of their financial future. When they get more mindful and intentional, anxiety goes away, they feel good about their habits in the present, and they have the assurance that they're heading in the right direction. The same goes for you, as you continue on this journey.

Chapter Summary

Your income isn't just your paycheck. Income means money coming in from all directions, including bonuses, gifts, dividends, pensions, sales of assets, side hustles, and more. This income is then used in relation to one's expenses to calculate and compare your income vs. expenses. This number helps you understand whether you have a deficit you need to address or a surplus you can leverage toward greater net worth. When you think of income intentionally, you begin to see more opportunities and have the freedom to increase it.

 | **KEY TAKEAWAYS**

- Income is only one piece of the financial puzzle. Having a high income does not mean wealth.
- Income includes all money coming in, not just wages and salary. There are many possibilities to increase income beyond wages and salary.
- Shift to becoming more mindful and intentional with your income and consider it a tool to increase your net worth. Seek opportunities to boost your income.

CHAPTER 5:

Your Expenses

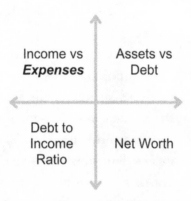

Income vs **Expenses**

Assets vs Debt

Debt to Income Ratio

Net Worth

There are four primary measures of your financial snapshot:
1. Income vs. **Expenses**
2. Assets vs. Debt
3. Debt-to-Income (DTI) Ratio
4. Net Worth

Expenses are the second half of your income vs. expenses equation. To determine whether you have a surplus (income exceeds expenses) or a deficit (expenses exceed income), subtract your expenses from your income. To do that, you need to learn how to calculate your expenses.

I'm excited to share this material with you. For many people pursuing greater financial health, this is where the rubber meets the road. The lessons I've taught so far begin to feel real as they look at their actual numbers and come up with one of the numbers they need for their snapshot. In this chapter, we'll cover the second half of the first equation, which will determine whether you're running a monthly deficit or a surplus. Your financial snapshot will become clearer.

This is also where I cover topics like needs vs. wants, fixed vs. flexible expenses, the importance of each purchase in relation to our goals, and emotional spending. All of these variables are important and must be taken into account for personal financial planning to be successful. If you make a plan to reduce your expenses, but it eliminates all of your wants, you'll lose a great deal of life satisfaction. This is not healthy and could be counterproductive by creating an emotional spending spree.

Expenses take more calculation than income. Income can come from a variety of sources, as covered in the previous chapter, but you won't have as many income sources as expenses. Every time money goes out of one of your accounts, for any reason, that's an expense. As you can imagine, your expenses could be in hundreds of different categories throughout the year. Because of this, there will be more charts in this chapter, and you will have more work to do in recording and analyzing your average monthly expenses.

Don't worry, you can work through these exercises together via the charts in your Companion Guide to find your total monthly expenses. Then, you'll categorize them into the aforementioned needs vs. wants, fixed vs. flexible, importance of the purchase to you, and your emotions when you made the purchase. This will help you more easily see which expenses you can reduce or areas to strategize if you have an income vs. expenses surplus.

Some expenses will be easy to figure out and track. This includes fixed expenses like a mortgage, a car payment, or student loan repayments—those expenses that do not change every month. Your variable, or flexible, expenses—those expenses that change every month, such as food, utilities, clothing, etc.— will be more difficult. I have created a monthly expenditure record for you to make this process simple and less time-consuming.

You can do this! I know that if it takes too much of your time to track these expenses, you won't do it, so I kept that in mind in developing the expense record. Tracking your expenses in detail allows you to see where your money is spent, carefully analyze your spending, identify poor spending habits, and determine your budget leaks. Budget leaks are those expenses you are unaware of leaking out of your account. Knowing where you spend your money is a crucial component of your financial snapshot. Without it, you won't be able to accurately move forward.

As you analyze your expenses, you may see things you want to cut immediately. Remember, I'm not asking you to drink tap water and eat inexpensive noodles every day for the next five years. Instead, you have to determine which trade-offs you're willing to make and the opportunity costs you're willing to incur. These are two vital concepts to know when analyzing your expenses.

Trade-Offs and Opportunity Costs

You can't have it all. People often get into debt because they buy items they can't afford—or simply buy everything they want. To become mindful and intentional with your expenses, you need to start thinking of trade-offs and opportunity costs.

A **trade-off** means compromising on something you want in order to get something else. Every transaction is a trade-off if you think about it. For example, if you choose to eat out for lunch and spend $10, that is a trade-off. You could have spent that $10 on something else and acquired lunch through eating at home. Now, you don't have that $10 for anything else.

Opportunity costs are potential benefits that you lose when choosing one option over another. You can think of it as the economic value of the choice you *didn't* make. For example, say you have $1 million to invest. You choose to invest it into a product line that generates a return of 5 percent. If you could have spent the money on a different investment that would have generated a return of 7 percent, then the 2 percent difference between the two alternatives is the forgone opportunity cost of this decision.

These two concepts are why cutting expenses and raising your income isn't always simple. As you consider your own expenses, consider the trade-offs you are making, the ones you can make, and the opportunity cost for the decisions you have to make.

How to Track Your Expenses

Tracking your expenses in detail allows you to see where your money is spent, carefully analyze your spending, and identify poor spending habits. Reviewing your expenses after one month allows you to carefully analyze your spending and evaluate whether it was necessary.

Spending Charts are available in the Companion Guide or on the website. If you wish, you can create your own spending chart simply by tracking your expenses and placing them in spending categories.

Determine Your Income vs. Expenses

Coming up with your income vs. expenses is very simple if you've followed the process so far. Simply take the average monthly income you calculated in the last chapter and subtract the average monthly expenses you just determined. It will give you one sum or difference, detailing your surplus or deficit.

If the number is positive, congratulations, you have a monthly surplus. If it's negative, you have a monthly deficit. Many students completing this exercise had no idea how much they really made or spent each month, and they found themselves with a deficit, or at least close to one.

Whatever your number, positive or negative, you will have some financial decisions to make, involving overcoming a deficit and leveraging your surplus. Below are the big-picture strategies to use. Also covered are adjusting spending and increasing income in greater depth in chapters 10 and 11, respectively:

Strategize Your Deficit

If you have a deficit, don't panic. You're aware of it, and you get to choose how to respond. At this time, you can shift from being reactive to proactive.

You may have had a sinking feeling during the past two chapters. You had an inkling that your expenses exceed your income because you've been putting things on the credit card and not keeping track of those expenses. It seemed like no matter how much you made, you didn't have anything left over—or you spent any extra money whenever you had it.

If you do have a deficit, meaning you spend more than you earn, you have two options.

1. Make more money.
2. Spend less money.

It's simple, but not easy. You either need to reduce your spending or increase your income—or a combination of the two. Thankfully, you have the power and freedom to do both.

First, analyze your spending habits. Find the leaks in your budget. Look at your spending chart and determine what isn't important that you spend money on. Are there unimportant wants you can eliminate this month? Start with expenses that aren't important, aren't emotional, and are flexible as opposed to fixed. These are the easiest to reduce or eliminate. Often these include subscription services you don't use, luxuries that don't help you toward your target, and hobbies you could reduce.

You can also find less expensive alternatives for your needs. Maybe you can get by with half the money you currently spend on food or transportation. This often looks like cutting out restaurants, being conscientious about using your gasoline, or using public transportation for a time.

Additionally, you can simultaneously increase the amount coming in. Last chapter, we talked about quick ways to boost our income. This could look like taking overtime, adding a side gig, applying for a second job, and selling items you don't need.

[Use the chart in the Companion Guide to help formulate a strategy around the most common line items: Housing, Utilities, Transportation, Food, Insurance, Work, Health, Fitness, Children, Pets, Personal, Household, Debt, Savings, Gifts, Entertainment, Education, and Miscellaneous.]

For each expense, you will document your current expense, the amount reduced, the adjusted expense, and the strategy to reduce spending in that category. A *Surefire Approach to Slash Your Spending* that includes over one thousand tips on reducing spending in each expense category is available for free on the Anchord. money website.

Again, you'll also find more in-depth strategies in chapters 10 and 11.

Strategize Your Surplus

If income exceeds expenses, congratulations!

Still, you need to strategize your surplus. You're doing well with managing your resources, and now it's time to optimize that amount to get toward your goals. Otherwise, the surplus will disappear into mindless spending and budget leaks.

Look at which areas of the eight areas of life you want to improve and how money relates to them. Make sure your importance ranking on each expense lines up with this. This will enable you to set your long-, intermediate-, and short-term goals, and use your surplus accordingly. Note: If you have credit card debt, you should not consider it a surplus and chunk that money into that debt. Every strategy must involve paying down credit card debt. Because of the interest rate, it drains you in the long run. So getting rid of this credit card debt will improve both your surplus and your net worth in the long run.

One semester in our class, students were working on their spending analysis and balancing their budget. I was working with one particular student who had a very good financial picture, with her monthly income outpacing her expenses. I praised her for that, and she responded with, "I do have credit card debt, but I'm not paying on it, so I didn't include it." I asked whether her parents or someone else was taking responsibility for that debt, and she said, "No, I just don't pay it." I had a conversation with her explaining that she does need to make good on that debt because it will come back to haunt her, probably sooner than later. At that time, I was more worried about her debt than she was.

[Use the chart in your Companion Guide to prioritize your options.]

The options include paying down or paying off credit card debt, establishing or adding to your emergency fund, adding additional money to your retirement, designating money toward a short-term goal, designating money toward an intermediate-term goal, designating money toward a long-term goal, paying extra money toward a mortgage or other loan, and saving for a vacation, wedding, etc.

This is by no means an exhaustive list, but it can get you started on the right path. Leverage your surplus to benefit your financial picture in the long run!

Although I'll go into more detail in chapter 10, here are a few questions you can think about when it comes to being more mindful of your spending right away:

- How will/did this purchase improve my life?
- Will this purchase matter ten years from now?
- Does this align with my money values?
- Will this purchase bring me peace, or will it make me feel guilty?
- Does this purchase get me closer to achieving my goals, or is it an emotional purchase?

The answers to these questions will give you the perspective you need to make decisions aligning with your strategy. Ideally, expense tracking should last for one year. This will enable you to record all your monthly, quarterly, and annual expenses. The more you do this, the easier it will get. You won't have to be as detailed as you go further.

Strategies to reduce expenses in each product category are available for purchase on the website. While this is not an exhaustive list, it will give you some ideas on spending reduction.

It's Like a Health Checkup

Now you have one piece of the puzzle to form your financial snapshot. Over time, moving from a deficit to a surplus, or a surplus to a greater surplus, will improve your financial future. Whatever information you've gained through this exercise, now you know the truth, and you have been empowered to take steps toward growth.

It's like a health checkup. Completing this financial health checkup and finding a surplus is like going to the doctor and discovering that you are healthy, and all is good. From there, you'll want to maintain your health and improve. This means purposefully examining what you're doing right and what you can build upon.

If the number is unhealthy, it's like the doctor pointing out a couple of areas of concern in your health. The doctor will then give you some advice on how to get aggressive and targeted with improving those numbers. In the same way, when you have a deficit, you need to intentionally increase your income and reduce your expenses.

I would recommend repeating this process each month for at least one year. It will get easier over time, and you'll also be able to track your progress. When my students diligently follow this process, many of them are able to move from a deficit into a surplus in a matter of months. This gives them the power to pay off debts and move toward increasing net worth.

Chapter Summary

This chapter gave you a system for tracking your expenses to come up with a monthly total. You tracked your expenses based on the type, amount, wants vs. needs, fixed vs. flexible, importance of the purchase, and emotions felt when purchasing. This allows you to conduct an analysis of your spending vs. income and determine whether you have a surplus or deficit.

What to do about this surplus or deficit relating to the items on the spending chart was covered. This gives you your income vs. expenses, and some tactics for improving it over the short and long term. With this information, our financial snapshot has become clearer. Now, we're ready to move into assets and debt.

 KEY TAKEAWAYS

- Tracking your expenses is crucial to move forward in developing a financial plan that you can stick with.
- Determining trade-offs and opportunity costs is essential to mindful and intentional spending.
- Strategize how you will best leverage a surplus or deficit.
- To be more mindful and intentional, with every purchase, ask yourself how the purchase will improve your life, whether it will matter ten years from now, whether it is aligned with your values, whether it gives you peace, and whether it helps you move toward your financial goals.

CHAPTER 6:

Your Assets

Income vs Expenses | **Assets** vs Debt

Debt to Income Ratio | Net Worth

Remember the four primary measures of your financial snapshot:

1. Income vs. Expenses
2. **Assets** vs. Debt
3. Debt-to-Income (DTI) Ratio
4. Net Worth

This chapter covers the first half of your assets vs. debt equation.

Sorting through your loved one's belongings is a somber moment. It is very overwhelming. We acquired an overabundance of possessions as a result of deaths in our families. That created quite the task to go through. As we picked through the items, we naturally began sorting them into a few categories:

- Some of them were sentimental items that we chose to hold onto and pass them down along the generations.
- Other items were somewhat valuable in the monetary sense, but not sentimental. These included collectibles, furniture, and some electronics. We put these aside to either sell or give away.
- Finally, most items had neither sentimental nor financial value. For these, we had to complete many trips to secondhand stores to donate items and to the local dump for what they wouldn't take.

Why do I share all this? Because it puts the concept of our assets into perspective. There are a variety of definitions of the word "assets" around. To me, it means possessions in our name that contain value. And frankly, there are also plenty of possessions we have that don't have value. That's where mindfulness comes into play. Add up the value of all these items to calculate your **assets vs. debt**.

Along with income vs. expenses, your assets vs. debt colors in your financial snapshot. It lets you know where you're at now, so you can make decisions about how to move forward. These two numbers combined tell you your **net worth trajectory**, whether it's increasing or decreasing over time. No matter your particular financial goals, I haven't met an individual who wants their net worth to decrease over time!

What Are My Assets?

Let's take the definition of "possession that contains value" and run with it. Under this definition, your assets can be physical possessions that you hold the title or deed of ownership for. These include items like homes, cars, and collectibles. In fact, that's often the first thing that comes to mind when someone hears about "assets." While they don't give the full story, these assets do matter greatly.

For example, one asset to own is real estate, especially a home in a good location. This is because property tends to increase in value, or **appreciate**, over time. So, when you buy a house, even with a home loan, it boosts your net worth trajectory.

However, you can think smaller in terms of your assets too. There are plenty of possessions lying around your home, some of which have monetary value. Everything you own is a kind of asset—though its value may be zero or very close to it. From the clothes in your drawers to the drawers themselves, they count toward your total assets.

Assets can also be abstract representations of value. For instance, the money in your bank account represents a value. Any stocks or bonds you own are also an asset. Having cash and money in the stock market increases the amount of monetary value you possess. I know I'm writing in more technical terms here, but it's important to be able to unpack these concepts precisely. It allows us to put it more simply and know what we're saying.

Here's the simplified definition: Your total assets are the amount of money you would have if you sold everything. If you got rid of absolutely all of your possessions and sold all of your securities, how much would you end up with? That is your total assets.

Asset Types

I like to categorize assets into three main categories because it helps us see at a glance how they serve our financial vision. It all comes down to the value they contain over time.

1. Appreciating

As I just mentioned, when an asset appreciates, that means it goes up in value over time. The classic example is a house in a good area. However, this could include rare collectible items like baseball cards or action figures, classic cars, and bonds. If your assets appreciate more than they depreciate, it will increase your net worth (as long as your income vs. expenses is a surplus).

2. Depreciating

This is the opposite of appreciating. Assets that depreciate decrease in value over time. The classic example here is that new car that loses value as soon as you drive it away from the dealership. However, most of your possessions decrease in value over time, from your electronics to your furniture to your hobby equipment. That's vital to remember because you could inadvertently cause your net worth to decrease by investing in assets that lose value.

3. Consumed

Very few people think about consumed assets. These are assets that lose their value completely shortly after their purchase. The gasoline in your car, the food in your pantry, or even the paint you buy for the exterior of your home. These are very closely related to your straight-up expenses, but it's worth noting they do hold value between the moment you purchase them and the moment you use them. This is as opposed to a doctor's bill or a gym membership, which are not assets because there's no way to liquefy their value.

Calculating Your Total Assets

To determine your total assets, take a look at everything you own. Examples include the following:

- Real estate (property and houses)
- Securities (stocks, bonds, CDs, etc.)
- The money in your bank accounts
- Your cash on hand
- Your vehicles and recreational vehicles
- Valuable possessions
- Collectibles and vintage furniture

You also need to determine the **fair market value** of everything that isn't liquid. Liquidity is how quickly the item can be turned into cash. You can determine fair market value in a number of ways, depending on the asset. For houses, vehicles, and possessions, you might check listings for similar items on real estate listings, car sales websites, and digital marketplaces. For your bank accounts, it's as simple as opening your account view or calling the bank. Lastly, most people can determine the value of their securities at a glance online, depending on their plan. For more complex investment plans, it may require speaking to one's portfolio manager or financial advisor.

Total assets are the single dollar amount after adding everything up. It forms one-half of the equation for your net worth. Take the time to get that number for yourself.

My total assets are worth $_____.

[Use the Companion Guide to calculate your total assets.]

Purpose of Assets

Now that the definition and varieties of assets have been established—and you know how much yours are worth—let's take a step back. *Why have assets at all?* How do they fit into the picture of mindful and intentional money?

Besides being half the equation to determine your assets vs. debt (and therefore your financial snapshot), assets are meant to serve you. Every asset you own serves some purpose, even if it's just to get you from point A to point B. However, a mindful and intentional person uses assets to *grow their financial future.* They have a tremendous capability to grow our net worth if we can take advantage of appreciation and compound interest.

Appreciation and Compound Interest

If you've looked into investing before, you may have heard the analogy of the doubling penny. It's the classic question: Would you rather have $2 million right now, or a penny that doubled in value every day for thirty days? If you aren't aware of the best answer, you might take the $2 million. It seems like there's no way the penny could be worth more, even if it doubles in value every day for thirty days. However, if you run the numbers, it paints a compelling picture:

Penny a Day Illustration

Day 1	$	.01	Day 16	$	327.68
Day 2	$	.02	Day 17	$	655.36
Day 3	$	.04	Day 18	$	1,310.72
Day 4	$	.08	Day 19	$	2,621.44
Day 5	$	.16	Day 20	$	5,242.88
Day 6	$	.32	Day 21	$	10,485.76
Day 7	$	.64	Day 22	$	20.971.52
Day 8	$	1.28	Day 23	$	41,943.04
Day 9	$	2.56	Day 24	$	83,886.08
Day 10	$	5.12	Day 25	$	167.772.16
Day 11	$	10.24	Day 26	$	335.544.32
Day 12	$	20.48	Day 27	$	671,088.62
Day 13	$	40.96	Day 28	$	1,342,177.28
Day 14	$	81.92	Day 29	$	2,684,354.56
Day 15	$	163.84	Day 30	$	5,368,709.12

That's right, the penny would be worth over $5 million on day thirty, much more than the $2 million. This is an example of compound interest.

Compound interest is extremely powerful and applies to certain assets. It also applies to most debts. Credit card debt compounds against you. The dollar itself slowly loses value over time, so if you don't get some kind of appreciation back for the dollars you invest, then inflation compounds against you too.

So a good use of assets is one that appreciates while you use it, like a house. A fantastic use of assets is one that gives you compound interest, like many retirement savings plans. However, depreciation and compound interest can work against you if you invest in the wrong assets or carry a large amount of debt. That will be covered more in chapter 8. For now, understand that assets have a tremendous impact on your financial situation, especially as years and decades go by. The younger you are when earning compound interest, the better the payout.

Depending on your short- and long-term goals, you may decide to leverage your assets for increased income or for increased net worth. For example, you may offload some assets to pay off high-interest debt, and then save up and invest in a house.

Use Assets to Increase Income

Leveraging your assets toward your income generally requires selling something. Some people decide to chip away at debt by selling off assets they don't need, or ones that don't appreciate over time. This could look like selling a new car and getting an older model that still fulfills their needs, then using the money earned to pay down a credit card. It could also mean downsizing a home. Many people find themselves paying more in rent or a mortgage for rooms and space they don't actually use. In fact, I know plenty of people who have rooms in their house just for storage! Going back to what I previously said about having too much stuff. Now, what if they sold those items and then got a smaller house? That would give them a boost to their income from the sale of those items while reducing their monthly housing expenses.

Remember, using assets to increase your income is a poor strategy if you have a deficit in your income vs. expenses. It will feel like you're shoveling cash into a hole. No matter how many assets you sell off, the extra income will get swallowed up by your monthly spending.

Use Assets to Increase Net Worth

One long-term strategy that benefits many people is to strategically invest in assets that appreciate and compound over time. By now, you've thought about where you want to be financially in ten, twenty, or thirty years. For most people, that goal will be to have a much higher net worth than they do now. To get there, you may consider investing in real estate and using it to profit you through selling it or renting it. Note that real estate is not an area that you want to get into without a significant amount of research and experience. You may also consider investing in a retirement savings account that offers steady, compounding growth.

Again, high income doesn't help if your net worth is decreasing. Net worth will decrease if expenses and the value of debt increase faster than the value of assets.

Eventually, all the extra assets you have will need to be sold to go toward paying off debt (this is scary to think about). So an intentional approach could be to improve your income vs. expenses, then use that extra income to pay down debt to improve your assets vs. debt, and then begin investing the surplus into appreciating assets.

Mindful and Intentional Assets

Everyone has different goals when it comes to their assets and overall finances. The key is to mindfully and intentionally move toward your vision. You can use your assets to do that. In fact, I would encourage you to begin asking yourself how each and every one of your assets serve your vision—and if it doesn't, consider selling or getting rid of it.

After going through the belongings of our family members, I resolved to do something different. Whether they intended to or not, they left us with a great deal of assets, many of which had no value. Did I want to have the same story? It caused me to begin looking at my assets and possessions differently. For each of my possessions, I asked the following questions:

- Do I want this?
- Would my kids want this if I passed away?

If the answer was "No" to either of those questions, it was time to sell or discard that possession.

Additionally, for our purposes, I would add a question:

- How does this asset serve my financial vision?

Every asset should get you closer to your goal, not trip you up or drag you in the wrong direction. Many people pay rent or a mortgage on extra rooms they don't use or have furniture payments on a couch they barely sit on. Others have closets full of clothes they're saving for "someday," even though fashion may change by the time they get to that day.

Lastly, having an enjoyable life both now and in the future is probably part of your vision. I'm not asking you to become ultra-minimalist and sell everything you don't use every day. I am saying, though, to put some thought into it: if you don't get enjoyment out of an asset, and it doesn't help your net worth trajectory, then maybe it's time to sell or get rid of it. Instead of telling you what to do, I'm inviting you to take a mindful approach to your assets.

Reducing your assets and leveraging them for your short- and long-term goals gives you plenty of opportunities to make positive movement toward your financial future. Plus, we have half the equation for the second equation of your snapshot. Now, we need to calculate our total debt. This will help you see both your income vs. expenses and your net worth.

Chapter Summary

Your assets are half of the equation for the second equation you need to calculate, your assets vs. debt. This essentially gives you your net worth. When you take this number and add your income vs. expenses, you can see whether your net worth is increasing or decreasing over time.

Assets come in multiple forms. I've categorized them in terms of appreciating, depreciating, and consumed. It's important to recognize when you buy or sell an asset what you want it to do for you in terms of the eight areas of life and your overall financial vision. This gives you a mindful and intentional approach to assets.

 | **KEY TAKEAWAYS**

- Asset types include those that appreciate, depreciate, or are consumed. To calculate your assets, total the dollar amount of everything you own.
- Compound interest is powerful and can work to your advantage with saving and investing, or to your disadvantage with your debt. The younger you are, the better the payout of compound interest with your saving and investing.
- Use assets to increase your income and net worth.

CHAPTER 7:

Your Debt

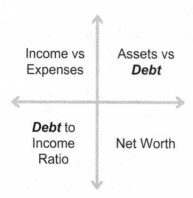

Income vs Expenses | Assets vs **Debt**

Debt to Income Ratio | Net Worth

t's review time again. Remember the four primary measures of your financial snapshot:

1. Income vs. Expenses
2. Assets vs. **Debt**
3. **Debt**-to-Income (DTI) Ratio
4. Net Worth

I had a desperate student tell me that he charged $2,000 to a credit card over the summer and his parents didn't know about it. I saw the terror in his eyes and the "boy, I really messed up" look. First, I reassured him that it was a fixable problem, and I was proud of him for addressing it. Together, we worked on a six-month plan that he felt confident he could accomplish. I told him that once the debt was paid off, I wanted him to tell his parents what had happened, that he'd got himself in debt, but he'd taken care of it and gotten himself out. He smiled and said he would. With money, it often takes situations like this to learn, and it was a wonderful teachable moment for this young person. Mom and/or Dad could have lectured him (and probably did) about credit card debt until they turned blue, but it wasn't until he actually experienced it that a lesson was learned.

In this section, we will cover the second half of your assets vs. debt picture. Once debt is calculated, we will be able to calculate our debt-to-income (DTI) ratio.

Debt, the big D word, can make a mess out of your financial picture. Debt can certainly have a bad reputation. However, I hope that through this section you will eliminate the fear and gain the mindfulness needed to make the right decisions around debt—not to mention get some tools in your hands to pay off your current debt.

Medical debt is one of the biggest reasons for bankruptcy. True story: A person went to the emergency room needing medical help. He was asked whether he had insurance, and he said, "Yes, money is taken out of my check each pay period for Medicare." The person was twenty-five years old and, much to his surprise, did not qualify for Medicare.

For many families, a small medical expense they weren't planning for can be difficult, if not impossible, to avoid. For those with recurring medical needs, like cancer patients and survivors, it can lead to higher levels of debt. These facts underline the importance of understanding and managing your debt.

As previously mentioned, debt gives us the second half of your **assets vs. debt picture**. When you add up your total assets, all the value you own, and subtract all the value you owe other people through liabilities, you're left with one number. This number is either positive or negative. Additionally, this number changes all the time as interest accrues on debt, debt gets paid off, and assets the individual owns either appreciate or depreciate.

Debt also lets you calculate your DTI, another angle to view your snapshot from. It doesn't need any additional numbers to calculate: it's your monthly debt obligations compared to your gross monthly income (before taxes), written as a percentage. Target a DTI of 36 percent or lower, with no more than 28 percent of that debt going toward servicing a mortgage or rent payment. For example, if your debt is $2,000 and your gross monthly income is $6,000, then your DTI is 33 percent.

Many young people start with a negative net worth. For example, a new couple purchasing a home will bring a large amount of debt that is higher than their current assets. People who have student loans and a car payment may have a negative net worth.

Others may have a positive net worth, and they want to know how to increase it. They want to know whether they should avoid debt at all costs, or if there are times when they should take on debt because of the long-term benefits. Both situations will be examined in this section.

But first, consider the age-old debate:

Good Debt vs. Bad Debt

People have a variety of opinions about debt. Your family of origin and faith could significantly affect your attitude to debt.

Additionally, people have natural predispositions toward debt that get further changed though their life experiences. Some people have a hard time taking on any debt at all and go to great lengths to avoid it. Others don't care about debt whatsoever and feel no stress about having a home loan, car loan, student loans, and credit card debt. Then there are those who fall somewhere in the middle of that spectrum. Plus, these attitudes might change when, say, it's time to buy a house and the individual has almost no recourse except a large home loan. In that case, the individual may learn to live with a debt that they were otherwise avoiding.

So is all this debt good or bad?

Well, let's unpack the question. First, what do I mean when I say good or bad? When I use those terms, I'm generalizing. I teach financial literacy, not ethics or philosophy. When I say good or bad, I typically mean the way that it impacts your financial picture in relation to your financial goals. Sometimes debt is useful for getting you where you want to go, and sometimes it's the exact opposite. So, if you see the words "good" or "bad" being thrown around in this book, don't think I'm moralizing or telling you what to do. I'm a neutral party here, giving you a simple plan to get to your vision, which incorporates your ideas of good and bad.

Sometimes debt is unavoidable and helpful in achieving goals. Know that this statement does not give you a green light to go out and charge a significant amount of money on a credit card. That is not what I mean. So when's a good time to take on debt, you might ask? The best example is buying a house.

Most people can't pay cash for a house. So they get a home loan with a mortgage, agreeing to pay a fixed amount each month for fifteen, twenty, or thirty years. Two types of loans are fixed and variable. A fixed rate stays the same throughout the life of the mortgage. A variable rate of interest gets periodically reassessed, making the payment fluctuate. The best option is to get the lowest interest rate at the shortest amount of time to pay it off.

If a home loan accrues so much interest, and puts a person in hundreds of thousands of dollars in debt, why should anyone ever buy a home? Because if you have a healthy financial picture and can pay your mortgage consistently, then you have a home that increases in value over time while you get to use it. By the time your mortgage ends, your home is likely more valuable than when the mortgage started. Plus, paying off the house significantly lowers your monthly expenses. If you rent, this is a monthly expense that you will pay your entire lifetime, which can be okay. Some people do not want the responsibility of owning a home and the necessary upkeep. Renting is a viable option to avoid homeownership.

Another example of "good" debt could be student loans. Understand that these loans are not to be used to increase your standard of living, but to pay for your tuition and essential needs while in school. A student in his second year of college spoke with me about his thoughts on leaving the four-year institution and going to a trade school. He had been taking out student loans to pay for his school thus far. He was quite perplexed when I explained to him that even though he left school without a degree, he was still obligated to pay back his loan for the full amount that he borrowed. This is true as well if you flunk out. Loan repayment is not based on getting a degree.

People go to college or university for a variety of reasons, but at its core, they want to get prepared for a certain job or career. If a student does well in college and gets a good job that requires their degree, then student loans are a worthwhile investment. It substantially increases their income for their entire career, and this income enables them to pay off the debt relatively quickly. A word of caution about overextending on your student loan debt: research degrees that are good returns on investment, in other words, degrees that lead to higher paying jobs that make sense taking out a student loan for.

On the other hand, there are plenty of examples of debt that serve the vision of almost nobody. Credit cards with high interest rates that were used to purchase non-essential "stuff" is bad debt. If you have a high interest rate loan on assets that rapidly depreciate, like a new car or boat, or even use a loan to pay for a vacation (that is immediately consumed), the debt you gain will probably not serve your financial vision. In these instances, it may be better to look at alternative means of getting what you need, like a less expensive car or public transportation, or determining whether you need that item at all. For example, you might wait to go on vacation until your credit card is paid off and you have a vacation fund saved up over time. Or you might postpone vacations and opt for staycations or less expensive options until your net worth is positive and increasing.

What does this all mean for the question of whether debt is good or bad? The simple answer is that it's not that simple. You can't put a huge stamp saying "GOOD" or "BAD" on top of all debt. Whether a certain kind of debt helps you or gets in your way depends on the eight areas of life you're targeting and the overall financial goals you have. Instead of making a blanket statement, you may consider the different kinds of credit and debt and determine which will serve you, if any.

Should I Use Credit and Go into Debt?

Here is a brief guide to help you make the decision for yourself on whether to use credit. There are several principles you should know and understand before making decisions about credit and debt. First, let's cover credit history and reports.

1. Understand Credit Reports

Loans and credit card purchases contribute to your credit history. Credit reporting companies gather information from your credit history into a credit report. A credit report includes all the information related to your bill payment history, public record information, credit applications, available credit, available credit used, timeliness of payments, and debt collector reports. All this information combines into your credit score, which lenders use to help decide whether to loan you money, in what amount, and for what interest rate.

Why Credit Reports Matter

In addition to loans, the information in your credit reports is used to make other kinds of decisions about you. For example, a poor credit history can make it difficult for you to

- Get hired
- Get and keep a security clearance for a job, including a military position
- Get an apartment
- Get insurance coverage
- Pay lower deposits on utilities and get better terms on cell phone plans
- Get a credit card

As you can see, having a poor credit history can make your financial life more difficult. Negative information on your credit report can appear on your credit report for seven years; however, bankruptcy can stay on your credit report for up to ten years. That's one reason it's important to pay bills on time and create a positive credit history. You also need to pay attention to the content of your credit reports. Since credit scores are calculated based on the information in the reports, take the time at least once a year to review the information in your report and make sure it's right. You can do this for free at AnnualCreditReport.com.

Hard inquiries are made by lenders after you apply for credit. These inquiries may affect your credit score. This is because most credit scoring models look at how recently and frequently you apply for credit.

Soft inquiries are reviews of your credit file when you have not sought to establish a new credit account. They include reviews of existing accounts by lenders, prescreening inquiries by prospective lenders, and your requests for your annual credit report. These won't affect your credit score.

Each of the three nationwide credit reporting companies—Equifax, Experian, and TransUnion—collects information about you to make their own credit report. So, if you have credit, you will likely have more than one credit report. To get a free credit report from these companies, go to AnnualCreditReport.com.

2. Understand Credit Scores

Credit scores come from the data in credit reports. A higher score makes it easier to qualify for a loan or lower interest rates.

Your credit score will vary depending on the company calculating it. Different companies use different information and formulas for calculating your scores. Scoring companies may also create different credit scores that are used when you apply for different types of credit.

As a result, you have more than one credit score. Banks, credit card companies, and lenders may use different credit scores to make decisions about offering you credit.

How Are Credit Scores Calculated?

Scoring companies have various mathematical formulas to calculate credit scores, typically starting with the information from your credit report. Two of the most commonly used credit scores are FICO (calculated using formulas from Fair Isaac Corporation) and VantageScore (calculated using formulas from VantageScore Solutions). Both companies have multiple versions of their scores, usually ranging from 300 to 850.

A FICO score above 700 is considered good by most businesses, and scores of 750 and higher are considered the best. There are five weighted variables that go into calculating your credit score. That means that some variables have a bigger impact on your score than others. They are

Payment history (35 percent) tracks whether you pay your bills on time. This is the biggest factor in your FICO scores. Paying bills late, not paying bills at all, and having bills that go to collections will lower your scores. Paying your bills on time may help increase your scores.

Amounts owed (30 percent) tracks what you owe, including debts you are paying down over time. It also includes your credit utilization rate; that is, how much of your available credit you're using. When the credit available to you decreases because you've used a portion of it and now owe money, your scores may drop.

Length of credit history (15 percent) tracks how long you've had credit accounts—the longer the history, the more positive effect on your scores. A long credit history provides strong evidence of how you use credit and patterns of your payment behavior.

New credit (10 percent) is tracked by measuring credit inquiries about you made by creditors and others. Too many inquiries may signal that you have a high demand for credit. Because this may indicate risk, your scores may drop. However, checking your credit score and report on your own doesn't affect the results.

Types of credit used (10 percent) are also considered. For example, your FICO scores may increase if you have both revolving credit (such as credit cards) and other types of credit, such as a mortgage or an auto loan that you repay in installments, in good standing. Generally, it's considered a good thing to have a mix of credit, such as a mortgage, an auto loan, and not too many credit cards.

3. Learn the Advantages and Disadvantages of Credit

Credit will help you get what you want now, but it will cost more in the long run. It makes purchasing more convenient, gives you a built-in record of transactions, and can help you with unexpected expenses. Plus, for housing, college degrees, and vehicles, credit may be helpful if not downright necessary. However, you will always end up paying more over time, and it has the potential to devastate your financial situation if you don't manage debt responsibly.

4. Know the Various Types and Sources of Credit

Loans for houses, cars, and higher education tuition have been discussed. Two common types of credit include

1. **Installment Loans:** These are a fixed amount of money that you borrow for a specific reason, like buying a house or car. The line of credit doesn't extend beyond the one purchase. These types of loans typically have a monthly payment.

2. **Revolving Credit:** This line of credit can be used over and over if you pay it off. As long as you stay under the credit

limit, you can use it for more purchases. The most common example of revolving credit is the credit card.

With revolving credit, you do not have to pay the balance in full each month; however, you will be charged extra money called **interest** or finance charges. Make every effort to fully pay this balance to avoid interest growing. Many people end up in debt because they misuse revolving credit.

5. Understand the Relationship Between Credit and Big Purchases

Some people use a credit card and pay it off consistently and in full to build their credit score. A good credit score can give you more favorable terms on a loan for a house or a car, resulting in lower interest and/or monthly payments. Other people reject credit cards entirely due to their high interest rates or the temptation to overspend.

6. Make Your Decision and Stick to It

While few people can live entirely debt-free (especially in their younger years), meaning no mortgage, no car loan, no credit cards, there is a wide spectrum of approaches. You must draw the line somewhere, and that somewhere depends on your individual goals. If you use credit for everything, it will ultimately lead to a negative and shrinking net worth, which will grow in momentum. Instead of a dream retirement or travel goals, you may find yourself working longer than you expected and in a situation where you can only afford the bare necessities.

Calculate Your Debt

As with your total assets, calculating your total debt is a relatively simple process. Sit down and take a deep breath. Many people avoid calculating their debt out of a fear of discovering how much they truly owe. However, you're committed to the process. You need to have a clear financial snapshot so you can get where you want to go in the future.

[When you're ready, complete the debt picture chart in your Companion Guide to list credit type, total amount owed, monthly payment, and the interest rate.]

After you complete the chart, add all the values in "Total amount owed." This will give you your total debt.

Assets vs. Debt

Now you can determine your assets vs. debt since you have calculated your total assets and total debt numbers. Simply subtract the total debt from the total assets. This gives you your assets vs. debt, which is essentially your net worth. Along with your income vs. expenses, it gives you a snapshot of where you are now.

For some people, the number will be positive. This means you have a positive net worth, which is helpful. If you had to, you could get out of all debt today by selling off assets. That's a feeling of financial freedom. Having a positive net worth and an income surplus makes it much easier to grow your net worth.

For others, the number will be negative. This means that if you sold everything today, you would still be in debt. In essence, you must work and earn more income. This could give you a mix of emotions depending on your financial background. Going from negative to positive net worth is usually a long-term process, so don't be too hard on yourself. If you can correct your assets vs.

debt and DTI, you can get to a positive net worth over time, giving you freedom and helping you reach your life goals.

[Record your calculations in the Companion Guide.]

Reducing Debt

For the rest of the chapter, I will discuss general strategies and two specific strategies for paying off debt. Remember when we set our long-, intermediate-, and short-term goals? If you find yourself with a negative net worth, then reducing your debt will most likely be one of your goals. Here are general tips for reducing debt:

1. **Pay more than the minimum due.** This will reduce the principal faster, which means you pay less in interest.

2. **Don't use credit to make ends meet.** If you need to borrow in order to pay your expenses, then your income vs. expenses is negative. Instead, focus on increasing your income and reducing your expenses.

3. **Always make payments on time.** If you miss a payment, almost all lenders will assess an additional fee. In other words, your debt will increase.

4. **Negotiate with creditors.** Creditors are more willing to work with you if you initiate contact with them and explain the situation. You might be able to negotiate a different payment plan, especially if you are proactive.

5. **Beware of companies that say they can fix your credit.** The only real way to pay off your debt is to pay off your debt. These companies may simply want you to transfer your debt over to them or charge you a fee for their services.

6. **Beware of teaser rates.** Sometimes companies offer low interest rates for a temporary window and then raise the rate much higher. Act as though there's no teaser and ask yourself whether you would still make that purchase.

In addition to these general tips, there are a couple of specific strategies you can use to pay off debt over the long term. They are the debt avalanche and the debt snowball. Here's a look at both options:

Debt Snowball vs. Debt Avalanche

There are a couple of methods that you can use to pay off debt. They both work! The important thing is buckling down and getting it done.

The **Debt Avalanche** means listing your debts by interest rate from lowest to highest, and then focusing on paying off your highest interest rate first.

The **Debt Snowball** requires listing your debts from the smallest amount to the largest, regardless of interest rate. You then pay your smallest debt first giving you a sense of accomplishment then moving on to the next smallest debt.

Which method you choose depends on your personality. Take a look at both options and the pros and cons of each, and then make a mindful, intentional decision on how to approach it.

Debt Avalanche

- **Step 1**: List debts from highest to lowest interest rate.
- **Step 2**: Make the minimum payment on all debt except for the one with the highest interest rate.
- **Step 3**: Pay as much extra beyond the minimum payment on this debt.
- **Step 4**: Once that debt is paid off, start using the money that you were paying and add this amount to the next highest interest rate. The payment on the new debt should be in addition to your current minimum monthly payment.

- **Step 5**: Repeat until all debts are paid in full!

[Use the chart in the Companion Guide to list your debt, interest rate from highest to lowest, the minimum monthly payment, and the extra dollar amount that will be added to this debt.]

This method saves you more time and money. You will pay off your debt in a shorter period with less overall interest. However, it requires more patience and discipline, as you will not experience the short-term motivation of seeing a debt totally disappear once it's paid off.

Debt Snowball

- **Step 1**: List debts from smallest to largest, regardless of interest rate.
- **Step 2**: Make minimum payments on all debts except the smallest.
- **Step 3**: Pay as much extra beyond the minimum payment on this debt.
- **Step 4**: Once that debt is paid off, start using the money that you were paying and add this amount to the next lowest debt. The payment on the new debt should be in addition to your current minimum monthly payment.
- **Step 5**: Repeat until all debts are paid in full!

[Use the chart in the Companion Guide to list your debt, total payoff from smallest to largest, the minimum monthly payment, and the extra dollar amount that will be added to this debt.]

This method helps to keep you motivated by having small victories; however, since you are disregarding interest rate, you are going to pay more interest using this method. Dave Ramsey's data shows that people are more likely to stick with a payoff plan using this approach.

Both methods work, so if you start with one and feel that it is not for you, changing your strategy is an option. Just keep moving forward and work on getting rid of that debt!

Planning for Debt

After you've considered all this content, what are your thoughts on credit and debt? Have they changed at all due to this material? How do your money scripts affect your view?

The answers to these questions will help you get a baseline for your personal debt plan. Consider your snapshot, where you are now vs. where you want to be in the future, and determine whether certain debts will help you get there.

Then, look forward. What major expenses do you anticipate in the next ten, twenty, or thirty years? Will you use credit to finance those expenses? Or will you be able to save up a fund for them? Develop the strategy now so that the debt doesn't surprise or stress you out—or so you don't have to go into debt at all.

At this point, you have three crucial equations for determining your financial snapshot. These are your income vs. expenses, your assets vs. debt, and your DTI. They tell us where we are today. The next chapter will dive deeper into what net worth is and how to get it on an increasing trajectory—something that will aid anyone's financial vision.

Chapter Summary

Debt is the second half of your assets vs. debt equation needed to determine your net worth. When you know how much you have in assets, and how much you have in debt, you get a positive or negative number closely representing your net worth. This is the second important equation in our financial snapshot after our income vs. expenses. Additionally, the DTI gives you another angle from which to view your snapshot.

Instead of thinking of debt as good or bad entirely, place it in the context of your overall desires, goals, and financial vision. Some debt might be useful for you that wouldn't help someone else on their journey, and vice versa. If you do find yourself with a great deal of debt, a good way to fix it is by correcting your income vs. expenses and then using the debt avalanche.

 ## | KEY TAKEAWAYS

- After calculating your overall debt, compare your assets vs. debt and your debt-to-income (DTI) ratio.
- Good and bad debt depends on your personal situation and goals. Which kinds of debt will serve you on this journey? Which will hold you back? Make the commitment to avoid taking on bad debt.
- Credit reports are used by lenders to determine your credit worthiness.
- Credit scores are based on payment history, amount owed, length of credit history, new credit, and types of credit used. This score ranges from 300 to 850 and impacts your ability to get credit as well as the interest rate that you will be charged.
- Determine strategies to reduce debt using either the debt avalanche or debt snowball method.

For more resources, visit Anchord.money.

CHAPTER 8:

Your Net Worth

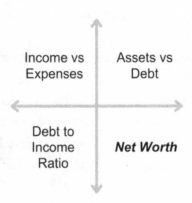

Income vs Expenses	Assets vs Debt
Debt to Income Ratio	*Net Worth*

Remember the four primary measures of your financial snapshot:

1. Income vs. Expenses
2. Assets vs. Debt
3. Debt-to-Income (DTI) Ratio
4. **Net Worth**

While we learned how to calculate net worth (the final primary measure of your financial snapshot) by subtracting your liabilities from your assets, I want to dive a little deeper into the topic. What do I mean by liabilities? Your liabilities are all your financial obligations, while your debts are obligations associated with outstanding loans. Though debts are often thought of when you think of liabilities, debts are really one subset of liabilities.

Ricardo and Jennifer drive the same exact car, down to the make and model. They also live in the same neighborhood. In the morning, they drive those identical cars out of their similar houses and go to the city. There, they work similar jobs, with the same salary and benefits.

Do Ricardo and Jennifer have the same net worth? Not necessarily. All that is shown so far is that they have similar income and assets. Those are respectively one side of two equations, income and assets, used for getting their snapshot, but now they need to find out their overall debt and expenses. Their debt will show their net worth, and their expenses will show whether it's increasing or decreasing.

Let's say that Ricardo saved up before buying the house and put 50 percent as a down payment. He has a remaining balance of $50K on the mortgage. Also, he rode the bus for a few years, and then bought a nice used car for cash. He has relatively little debt and fewer expenses in the form of a mortgage and car payment.

On the other hand, let's say Jennifer put 20 percent as a down payment on the home, still has $150K left on the mortgage, and is in fact leasing the car instead of owning it. In that case, she has greater debt in the form of the mortgage, greater expenses in the form of the lease, and the car she drives doesn't even count toward her assets!

In this case, Ricardo has the healthier financial snapshot, has greater net worth, and is likely improving his net worth over time. Even though their lifestyle appears the same, Jennifer's net worth is much lower and is definitely further away from reaching her financial vision than Ricardo.

What Is Net Worth?

Determining a person's net worth is kind of like looking under the hood of a car. Everything could look lovely on the outside, but the engine could have any number of problems. Our culture is materialistic. We want to "keep up with the Joneses" without realizing all the numbers you *don't* see.

For example, if you have $200K in assets, but $600K in liabilities, you're probably struggling way more than someone who has half the assets ($100K) as you, but no liabilities. That's how net worth is calculated. It's the same as our **assets vs. debt** from the previous chapter. If you followed those instructions, then you already have your numbers. Now, put all the equations together to get your snapshot.

Your Financial Snapshot

If you have a negative net worth and a negative income vs. expenses, you'll find no judgment here. I applaud you for working through the process to get an accurate picture of your finances, regardless of your finding. Now you need to diagnose the problem correctly before you work toward a solution, but it doesn't help you to dwell on guilt or shame about your financial situation; just work to improve it.

You started with your **income vs. expenses**. You determined this number by gathering all of your income sources, even the unconventional ones, and coming up with an average monthly income. Then, you did the same for all of your expenses, coming up with your average monthly expenses. By subtracting the expenses from the income, you came up with your number. A positive number meant a surplus, and a negative number meant a deficit.

Then, you moved into **assets vs. debt**. First, you took all of your assets and aggregated their fair market value to come up with your total assets. Then, you added up all of your debts to come up with your total debt. By subtracting the debt from the assets, you calculated your assets vs. debt. A positive number meant a positive net worth, and a negative number meant a negative net worth.

Now, look at those two equations to determine your trajectory. If nothing changes in your income, expenses, assets, and debt, what will happen to your net worth over time? The factors in this equation are your surplus/deficit, your net worth, and the types of assets you have. Your net worth will only grow over time if

- You have an income surplus
- You eliminate debt faster than it accumulates
- You invest your surplus into assets that appreciate

That will give you a positive net worth trajectory. No matter your starting position, if those three factors are true, you'll see success over time. If you take out one or two of those items, your net worth will stall or even decrease. Your net worth will decrease quickly if

- You have an income deficit
- You accumulate debt faster than you eliminate it
- Your assets depreciate faster than they appreciate

Complete Your Financial Report Card

With all that said, pay careful attention to your financial situation. Answer the following questions to get your full financial snapshot:

What is my monthly income vs. expenses? (Income minus expenses) _____

What is my net worth? (Assets minus liabilities) _____

Overall, are my assets appreciating (increasing) or depreciating (decreasing)? _____

Which is growing faster, my assets or my debt? _____

Am I accumulating more debt each month? _____

[Use the Companion Guide to complete your financial report card.]

The answers to these questions will give you your financial report card. They will show you the trajectory of your net worth. Are you on the right track? Remember, everyone has different financial goals and different areas of life they want to target. However, a positive and increasing net worth will greatly benefit you—that's why there is so much focus on it over the course of this section. To get to your financial vision, think more broadly than "I need to make more money," or "I need to pay off debt." Instead, it could help to think, "I need my net worth to increase over time."

Increasing Net Worth

To increase your net worth, it all starts with your **income vs. expenses**. Trying to improve your net worth while having an income deficit is like pouring water into a bucket with holes in it. No matter how much you try to conserve, water will pour out the bottom. To save and invest, you can't have more expenses than income. You'll end up using credit to cover your expenses and have debt that grows faster than your assets.

So the very first step involves getting to an income surplus. This was covered in depth in chapters 4 and 5. The long and short of it is this: You must increase your income, reduce your expenses, or both. For some, this looks like working a second job or a side gig while eliminating expenses and/or thinking of less expensive alternatives.

The next step is to pay off debts, especially ones with high interest rates. The interest accumulates against you, lowering your net worth over time. Most forms of high-interest debt will lower your net worth faster than assets will increase it. That's why I encourage students to pay off their credit card and follow the debt avalanche or snowball before diverting their income surplus into investments. There is some give and take here, as some liabilities can be paid off in a year or less, and others may take fifteen to twenty years, such as a mortgage. Plus, paying a mortgage itself is a means of reducing debt while growing one's assets.

The general rule? Pay off debt, save three to six months of expenses in an emergency fund, and invest 15 percent of your household income in appreciating assets like a house or a retirement savings plan.

This will increase your net worth over time—and remember, it will take time and effort. Your journey isn't the same as someone else's.

Reject Comparison

When you see Jennifer driving a nice car in a nice neighborhood, or posting on social media about her wonderful vacation, it could cause a mix of emotions. Some people might feel inspired, and others might feel negatively when comparing themselves to Jennifer. Many times, a question comes up:

"How can she do it?"

And frankly, a lot of times, the answer is "She can't." She has a life that seems enviable on the outside, but most Americans are living with thousands of dollars in debt, living paycheck to paycheck. The attractive car is actually leased. The picturesque home has turned her income vs. expenses upside down. The high-powered career came with hundreds of thousands of dollars of debt. If you think about it, your net worth could actually be higher than Jennifer's.

Oftentimes when my children were younger, we would drive by a nice house and one of the kids would say, "They must be rich." I would respond with, "Either that or they are in a lot of debt," helping them to understand that having material things is not always an indicator of wealth.

Maybe Jennifer has a seemingly great life right now (or she thinks she does), but she's charging purchases on credit cards, racking up debt, and her net worth is negative—and trending down. Sooner or later, her social media page will quiet down as she realizes she has to start digging herself out of a hole.

Statistics vary on a person's average credit card debt, but Intuit Credit Karma cites over $6,000 based on its 74 million members with credit cards.[4] As of the first quarter of 2023, Americans hold $986 billion in credit card debt.[5] That means that most of the people you see from day to day have to deal with high-interest debt, and many of their "possessions" aren't actually owned by them. Not that you'd be able to tell from the outside.

To sum up, we often buy unnecessary things with money we don't have to "impress" people we may or may not like. This does not make sense. Then the other side of the coin is people who are doing well financially. Sometimes, you'll see someone with a nice car and house, and they own them. Their net worth is positive and growing.

---

4   Ward, Paris. "Average Credit Card Debt by Age, Location and Credit Score." Credit Karma, April 20, 2023, www.creditkarma.com/insights/i/average-credit-card-debt.

5   "The Center for Microeconomic Data - FEDERAL RESERVE BANK of NEW YORK." Newyorkfed.org, 2023, www.newyorkfed.org/microeconomics/hhdc.html.

People who are millionaires can be just as stressed as people without money. Having more money doesn't automatically make your life calm and peaceful. While money can solve problems, it can also create problems. The more money you have, the more money you must manage. The good news is, you don't have to become more stressed as your income and net worth increase because you're laying the proper foundation now. You aren't just making money to make money, or to keep up with the neighbors; you're reaching the financial vision you set.

Your financial vision is yours and yours alone. You may think that someone else is further along than you on their financial future, but as you learned, that could be untrue, or they just chose to focus on different areas of life, different dreams, and a separate vision from your own. The only thing that matters is your personal destination and how you will get there. And you will get there.

Move toward Your Goals

A positive and growing net worth gives people a feeling of financial freedom, security, and satisfaction. They know that they can afford emergencies and pay off all their current debts. Plus, they likely have a nest egg growing for things like retirement, vacations, and legacy—not to mention an income surplus to give them the lifestyle they want now.

The destination is your **financial vision**. You determined that vision in the first section of the book when you looked at the eight areas that encompass life and wrote down goals for each. Then, you set short-, intermediate-, and long-term financial goals that match your overall desires. You know better than anyone where you're going.

Then, you determined where you are today. Plotting a course requires both a starting point and an ending point. This part of the book gave you your **financial snapshot** through determining your surplus/deficit and net worth. Now, you have a firm grasp on your current situation, and you committed not to judge yourself but to mindfully and intentionally improve your current financial situation.

That's where the next part comes in. The best way to get from point A to point B is to use a map. When you learn, plan, and execute this financial process, you'll start moving from your starting point (A) to your ending point (B). Slowly but surely, your financial vision will begin to come to life. It's an amazing feeling.

Chapter Summary

Your net worth is your assets (what you own) minus your liabilities (what you owe). It is not based on income. People with similar income and assets likely have a different net worth because they have varying levels of debt. Plus, their financial snapshot could be grim due to out-of-control expenses.

With your net worth and your income surplus/deficit, you can create a financial snapshot. It shows you how you're doing today, so you can move toward your financial vision. If you have an income surplus, appreciating assets, and no debt, your net worth will grow over time. That's your goal.

 | **KEY TAKEAWAYS**

- To increase net worth, eliminate debt and invest your income surplus into assets that appreciate.
- Setting goals will help you reach your financial vision— where you want to be.

- You now have your financial snapshot of where you are now. What do you think? Are you moving in the right direction?
- Reject comparison and make mindful and intentional decisions to begin moving toward your financial vision.

ANCHORD MONEY

Part 3:

LEARN, PLAN, AND EXECUTE

Now that we've talked about where you're going and discovered where you are today, it's time to learn, plan, and execute.

Let's take a step back for a minute. Remember what I told you in the beginning of the book? By reading this book, you will get

- Empowerment to become your best financial self
- A foundation that can strengthen your family and community in a domino effect
- Research-based information instead of anecdotes
- Multiple opportunities to engage with the content and make it personal to you
- A basic, nonintimidating process for financial success
- A plan that fits with your personality, habits, attitudes, and values instead of something cookie-cutter or built for someone else

- A custom financial strategy that leads to increased income, reduced expenses, paid-off debt, appreciating assets, and growing net worth
- A skill set to teach your children, or other young people in your life, how to develop their money management skills

At this point, you know the core financial concepts and strategies. Now, it's time to turn the vision and dreams into a reality.

You know your money scripts, personality, habits, attitudes, and values. You know the eight areas of life and which you want to improve the most. To do so, you've set long-, intermediate-, and short-term goals to accomplish.

You also have your financial snapshot. You have numbers for your income vs. expenses, your assets vs. debt, your DTI, and the trajectory of your net worth.

To sum up, you know where you're going, and you know where you are. Now, it's time to bridge the gap between those two. This means learning, planning, and executing a personal process for your financial success. To do so, you need to commit to a change, set yourself up for success, and implement strategies to improve your spending and earning. In the following pages, we'll pull everything together. You will take what you've learned so far and create a strategy to execute your plan.

Is your current method for managing your money working? Will your current path get you to where you want to go? If not, a change will need to be made. If you aren't sure how to do it, that is why you are here. You need to LEARN a different approach that works for you. You must also learn and understand your current money management behaviors and why you are doing them so that you know what you need to fix.

Once you learn, you need to change your current habits and money management routines—that aren't working for you—and develop a PLAN of action—a new approach. What major and minor tweaks can you make—habits you will need to break?

Now you need to make it happen—EXECUTE. Start implementing strategies to make your behavior change. The best-laid plan doesn't matter at all unless you execute, making your dream come to reality one step at a time.

We'll break this process down into the following steps: setting yourself up for success, mindful and intentional spending, making more money, and building muscle memory to make your future success automatic (and less painful). It will allow you to learn, plan, and execute your personal process.

CHAPTER 9:

Setting Yourself Up for Success

Several years ago, I taught a graduate-level class related to financial literacy. I noticed that each week, the same student would come up to me and say, "My husband and I discussed [topic related to my lecture the week before]" and would continue explaining to me their full conversation.

This went on for several weeks, and I finally looked at her and said, "I think that we saved a marriage." She looked at me and said, "You have no idea." I smiled, we both got teary-eyed, and she walked back to her seat. That was many years ago. I have often thought of that student and her situation and hoped that they were able to work out their differences and set themselves up for success.

All the best-laid plans often go awry. To put that in modern terms—life happens.

As of now, you have the groundwork and a solid foundation for financial success. You've set financial goals for your short-, intermediate-, and long-term financial picture. You've also learned where your finances sit today through your income vs. expenses, assets vs. debt, debt-to-income ratio, and net worth. Now, it's time to begin moving toward your destination.

I hope through this process that you have become more connected with your money and how you manage it. Like my student above, you've probably never sat down and discussed finances. They were having marital problems, but it seemed that after discussing their finances, it calmed some conflict in their marriage. My goal for you is not to just learn more information about money but to become more mindful and intentional about money in general. This gives you the power to move from chaos to calm in your financial life—not just gain knowledge.

So you want to be intentional as you begin to learn, plan, and execute a personal process for financial success. It requires stepping back and looking at the plan itself. Is it realistic and sustainable? In other words, is it something you can stick with?

When you decide to turn your finances around, you are excited and motivated, and as a result, may make huge and unrealistic goals. This attempt to change everything at once will likely not be sustainable, and you will be setting yourself up for failure.

Instead, make your plans work in the real world—your real world. Instead of changing everything all at once, consider your **trade-offs** and **opportunity costs**. It is a mistake to make things too painful for yourself at the beginning of this process. Cutting any expense that isn't strictly necessary will lead to resentment of the whole process. Instead, be intentional from the very beginning to make deliberate changes in your spending and income. Consider what you can trade instead of what you can cut. For every road you *don't* go down, consider the value of changing course and going down it. This will enable intentionality in your financial success plan.

You also need to be mindful. Many financial plans remove emotions from the equation. A plan that doesn't take emotions into account is set up for failure. So consider the emotions involved in reducing expenses, increasing income, and managing your financial picture. This will include a discussion of emotional spending, one of the primary causes of budget leaks that threaten to capsize your financial plan the most.

The rest of this book will talk about financial mind mapping, emotional spending, strategies for mindful and intentional spending, making more money, and building muscle memory to help you make your new financial plan a habit and less stressful.

Let's start with creating a visual of your financial map.

Financial Mind Mapping

A picture is worth a thousand words. A financial mind map will create a picture of your current financial situation and future goals. When you sit down to think about your finances, the thoughts can become jumbled. It can be easy to think about the most pressing needs, or the areas that cause the biggest emotional response, instead of considering the big picture. So the mind map forms that big picture. Being able to see everything at a glance gives you the precious power of detachment. You get a bird's-eye view of your finances. This is the same as goal setting; they are jumbled in your head until you sort them out and write them down, in detail.

Income, expenses, and goals will be neatly categorized. It will also reveal helpful information. If you find that creating your map is complicated, then there's too much going on in your finances. Use it as an opportunity to simplify.

It can also show an unbalanced picture of your finances. If your mind map has a ton of entries in the expense category but very few in the savings and investment category, that could be a sign to focus on paying off the debt and opening a new savings stream.

The following is an example of a financial mind map:

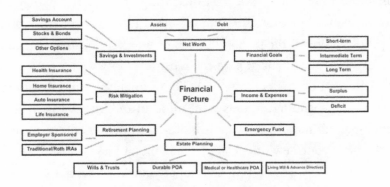

[Use the Companion Guide to create your own financial map.]

Looking at your financial picture at a glance will not only reveal unbalanced areas but also glaring holes. The example above lists "insurance coverage." If you wrote something similar on yours, but you don't have life insurance, that would be a hole. Or perhaps you noted that you want to save for car repairs, but when you look at your monthly budget, there's nothing allocated toward it. Having a visual financial plan will give you the action steps you need to move forward mindfully and intentionally.

It's all about moving forward. Everyone has their own starting point, plan, and pace. Some people will perform these exercises and immediately enter attack mode. They will get aggressive with their monthly expenses and pick up a second job for a span of months so they can "right the ship" in their finances. Then, it will flow into a more permanent, day-to-day plan.

Others will not have such an aggressive plan in the beginning but adjust with a smaller intensity. They may have circumstances in their life preventing them from making drastic moves at the beginning, but they will still make progress. You can turn a ship around by moving the rudder only one degree to the side; it just takes longer. However, a long process of small tweaks may lead to greater commitment and less shock to the system.

Savings Options

The students I teach don't always have a plan for long-term savings and investments. When you make your financial mind map, look at what you have for savings and investments. If you don't have much, or are curious about what's out there, take a look at these options:

1. High-Yield Savings Account

A high-yield savings account operates similarly to a regular savings account, but it has a much higher return, even up to 5 percent annual yields or more. Your existing bank may offer these accounts, but they are also available online.

2. Certificate of Deposit (CD)

CDs earn interest on what you deposit if you don't touch the money for the duration of the term. They can also earn higher yields than traditional savings accounts. Most banks have a CD option for you.

3. Money Market Account

Money market accounts operate similarly to a bank account, with interest, debit cards, and check writing. However, they may have minimum balance requirements, additional fees, and rules regarding transactions.

4. Checking Account

A checking account is a liquid account at a bank that typically doesn't offer interest. However, there are fewer restrictions on the minimum balance, fees, and transactions.

5. Treasury Bills

These are bills the US government auctions to fund various projects, sold at a discount and paid back at face value over a certain time period, depending on the interest rate. They are a secure form of short-term investment.

6. Short-Term Bonds

Bonds are similar to Treasury bills but can be purchased from other entities than the government. They typically give a fixed income, where you lend a certain amount of money and get an agreed-upon amount back after a term.

7. Investments (Stocks, Real Estate)

As opposed to bonds, stocks and real estate are not fixed. They can go up and down in value over time. Though some safeguards exist, there is always a risk. However, these investments can also grow exponentially over time.

The key when it comes to savings is sticking to the plan. This requires commitment from you to mindfully and intentionally change your current behavior to align your values and goals. Beyond completing the exercises in this book, and committing to a vehicle for savings, it means making those small decisions, day in and day out, to move toward your destination.

Money, Divorce, and Coparenting with Dr. Jill Bowers

Many people begin seriously looking at their finances due to a life event like a separation or divorce. Dr. Jill Bowers is a professor and coparenting expert who has performed research on divorce and coparenting education programs for the past fifteen years. This includes research with children of divorce, program review of coparenting education programs, and creation of a coparenting education program of her own.

She reports that couples in medium- or low-conflict divorces who agree on everything else still tend to disagree about finances. Financial stressors are one of the biggest stressors for parents going through a divorce. There are a lot of fears surrounding finances, which can lead to anxiety and depression.

Many couples are used to two incomes, and the divorce means they are now going to one. They also have the costs associated with the divorce itself, like mediation fees, attorney fees, and moving expenses. Some couples have to divide their assets like rental properties, retirement accounts, and savings accounts. This leads to many people going through a divorce and not coming out ahead financially, which is something to be aware of.

There is also the matter of children. How do you coparent well when it comes to money? Dr. Bowers had this to share:

1. Create a budget before agreeing to anything in divorce or separation. Strategize for expenses that don't exist yet. For example, these could be expenses related to sports and extracurriculars that you don't often think about when a child is too young for school.

2. Don't just "be nice" to protect the coparenting relationship but get agreements to safeguard your finances and your children. Your relational dynamic will change anyway.

3. Get your agreement into legally binding writing. Determine what the expenses are and who pays for what.

4. Plan for emergency contingencies, like losing your insurance due to a job transition.

The bottom line, according to Dr. Bowers, is that if you are okay financially, your kids will be okay. Some parents may feel guilty about the divorce and try to give their children anything they want or buy things to overcompensate. Dr. Bowers advises against that. You are comanaging expenses related to children, but you are not comanaging finances anymore. It's your individual responsibility. If you haven't had to manage your own finances, it's time to begin building a strategy for it for your future and for your children.

Understanding Emotional Spending

I am not an emotional spender. I am not an emotional spender. Wait, maybe I am an emotional spender! Did you know that 90 percent of spending is triggered by emotions and only 10 percent is from logic? Think about that for a minute. Many purchases occur because of some level of emotion, whether it be happiness, achievement, sadness, anger, guilt, jealousy, or fear. This is why I include the emotion category when tracking expenses: to help you determine whether an emotion triggered the purchase.

Why is the topic of emotional spending here when we have an entire chapter devoted to mindful and intentional spending coming up? It is included here because of how common I've found it as an obstacle for people in their financial journey. Simply put, if you want to set yourself up for success, you need to understand and mitigate emotional spending.

What is emotional spending? It means spending money during periods of heightened emotion, on things that you don't really need or want. Shopping sprees and impulse buys fall under the category of emotional spending. You may have heard of the term "retail therapy," meaning someone navigates or copes with pain or trauma through shopping. Retail therapy is a very real thing, but it doesn't have to be demonized. Many people might find retail therapy valuable if it fits in their budget and doesn't create debt. I'm not saying to never have any retail therapy again for the rest of your life; I'm saying that it must fit within your overall financial picture.

Emotional spending is compounded by the number of options you have as a consumer. Say you want to go to the store to buy shampoo because you've run out. If you go to one of the big-box stores, you'll see an entire aisle of hair products to choose from, hundreds if not thousands of shampoos. They claim to increase volume, restore dry and damaged hair, help oily hair, eliminate dandruff, detangle, protect color, create shine, thicken thin hair, nourish, moisturize, and on and on and on. And that doesn't even get into the different scents that are available. It's overwhelming. If selecting a shampoo is exhausting, I encourage you to not visit the baby aisles. For something so little, the number of products to choose from is ridiculous. This overwhelming feeling often leads to emotional spending.

Any time there is a change, it can cause stress. The idea of going on a financial improvement journey can be overwhelming to where you might be tempted to mitigate the emotional response with emotional spending. In other words, the very thing you are trying to avoid comes to reality. That's why it's included in the discussion of setting yourself up for success.

To overcome emotional spending, you need to determine whether this is something you do and more importantly how often, then learn how to navigate through the circumstances that trigger it.

Do You Feel That You Are an Emotional Spender?

Think about it. Do the descriptions of emotional spending above resonate with you? Some people will automatically say "Yes" and identify as an emotional spender. Others might have to consider it for a while. Here are a few questions to help clarify the matter:

Do you buy things to improve your mood? Emotional spenders feeling negative emotions or wanting to feel a positive emotion will often buy unnecessary items and ride that emotional high for a while.

Do you buy things to improve your confidence? For an emotional spender, the reason behind buying something isn't about their stated need, but an emotional reason underneath, a feeling of self-doubt.

Do you feel guilty after buying something? An emotional spending cycle can occur where the individual is triggered by an emotion, then buys something to cope with the emotion, only to feel worse after the purchase. If this is the case, returning the item to the store can quickly solve this problem.

[Use the Companion Guide to reflect and answer the above questions.]

It's okay if you're an emotional spender. We all buy things out of emotion sometimes, and emotions themselves are a vibrant part of life. A mindful and intentional plan doesn't discount our emotions or pretend they don't exist. Your plan should take your emotions into account. That's why spending out of emotions is okay, as long as it fits into your overall plan. There are times when emotional spending is okay; for example, when you want to treat yourself to something as a reward.

However, emotional spending becomes a problem when it happens frequently, creates debt, or causes relationship problems. It frustrates me when mental or financial health experts write emotions off and simply tell people to stop spending money. People who shop compulsively or have an addiction to spending money can't just stop. It's been recognized as a legitimate disorder, in which a person feels out of control. I compare an emotional spender to a person combating an addiction, such as alcohol and drugs. A twelve-step program is available for this person to recover. The strategy to improve emotional spending shouldn't be to simply say, "Stop spending money," but instead look at the root causes, triggers, and ways to overcome it.

Overcoming Emotional Spending
with Laura McRoberts

Laura McRoberts is a digital marketing consultant with a wonderful story about overcoming emotional spending.

Growing up, Laura began to believe that her value was associated with money and what she could bring to the table as a person. She doesn't know exactly where this started, but she remembers being influenced by the way her grandmother and mother thought about money. She felt afraid to disappoint the people in her life who mattered most.

In her first marriage, Laura remembers having a husband who did not take responsibility financially, and in fact, began to blame her after he overspent. He would tell her that she was stupid, and that she was the problem for financial issues. This led to an even deeper emotional response to the concept of money. Eventually, their thirteen-year marriage ended, and she became essentially a single mother with three children.

Not only had she picked up some unhealthy money habits, but the entire idea of money became filled with fear for her. When she met Jeff, who would eventually become her current husband, she couldn't talk about money with him. Whenever he would bring up money and want to sit down and talk about the budget, it would overload Laura's emotions. She felt like she was in trouble, like she was going to be told she wasn't good enough.

Laura got to a low place where she couldn't get help to pay for some of her expenses. Eventually, she used her employer's credit card to pay some bills she had and tried to hide it. She had full intention of paying it back but when payday came along, so did more bills. Soon, the business owner found out, filed charges, and Laura was arrested.

Laura still remembers having to tell Jeff, whom she wasn't married to yet, what had happened. Then having to tell her future stepchildren and her own children that she was going away for three years.

This led her to invest fully in counseling, which she had dabbled in previously. She also got into a twelve-step program and support groups. She began to untangle the belief that "money equals your value as a person." She started to understand that she can't control every situation and its outcome. The negative thoughts that lead to fear and hiding are not helpful and irrational.

Because of this, she began letting Jeff know how she felt and how her past marriage and upbringing had affected her. It led to them beginning to talk weekly about their budget without passing judgment on one another. Laura feels at peace knowing that even if she overspends or buys something she doesn't need, she isn't in trouble, and she and her family will be all right.

Laura's story shows how fear can be a huge trigger for emotional spending. It is why money can be so challenging for emotional spenders; it touches on some of our deepest pride and fears.

The good news is it can be overcome. You can get to a place where instead of money controlling you, you are controlling it. Where the amount of money in your bank account does not equal your value as a person. Your self-worth has nothing to do with your net worth.

For now, the first step is awareness. The next chapter will discuss strategies for mindful and intentional spending that will help you get a handle on your expenses, whether you identify as an emotional spender or not. Emotional spenders will find these strategies especially helpful, but everyone needs them as part of their personal process for success.

What does your financial mind map look like? Do you see imbalances on one side or another, or even holes to address? Take the time to think about the bird's-eye view of your financial situation before moving forward. Don't rush into an aggressive financial improvement plan without looking at the big picture. This is a huge piece of setting yourself up for success.

Next, determine whether you're an emotional spender. Out-of-control spending is the number one obstacle to reaching your financial goals. That's why it was included in this discussion. If you want your net worth to improve over time, it will not happen unless your income vs. expenses is a surplus. While making more money certainly helps (this is covered in more detail later), you should look at your expenses and spending first. If you can get your spending under control, it will make having an income vs. expenses surplus much easier.

If you have created a clear financial picture—your mind map—and you've identified the number one obstacle you're likely to encounter in your journey, then you're on the right track for success. Well done!

The next two chapters will dive deep into mindful and intentional spending and the practical ways to make more money. This will give you an income vs. expenses surplus that you can leverage into decreased debt and increasing assets. Together, decreasing your debt and increasing your assets will increase your net worth and propel you toward a strong financial future.

Chapter Summary

Before jumping into practical details, it is wise to set yourself up for success on the front end. To make sure you can plan and execute a personal process for financial success, you first need to learn about your financial map and emotional spending. This enables you to move forward mindfully and intentionally at the right pace. Some people will find it helpful to be more aggressive for a short time to fix their finances, and others will make small tweaks over a greater period of time. What matters is that you have a long-term commitment.

 KEY TAKEAWAYS

- A financial mind map is useful to create a picture of your current financial situation and goals.
- A variety of saving options are available to align with your risk tolerance and goals.
- Your emotions play an important role in managing your financial picture and account for 90 percent of your spending decisions.

- Whether you make aggressive or tiny changes in the next season, commit to improving your financial picture in the long term.

CHAPTER 10:

Mindful and Intentional Spending

Now that you've set yourself up for success by examining your overall financial map and the primary obstacle in your path, it's time to dive deep into your spending. When you attain control of your spending, it makes gaining a surplus in your income vs. expenses easier. This enables you to pay off debt and invest your money, increasing your net worth over time.

Changing how you use money requires small and sustainable lifestyle changes. I hope you can see that it's not about shocking your system by making multiple drastic changes all at once. Instead, think of it like a few deliberate pushes to get over a small hump. Once you get over the hump, you'll find momentum working in your favor.

Over the long term, simply being mindful and intentional about your spending, combined with setting SMARTER goals about your money, will create a healthier financial lifestyle that breeds success.

What Is Mindful and Intentional Spending?

Mindful spending is lifestyle-based money management that is aligned with your individuality. It is a more effective and sustainable approach to spending. If you build a budget that is not aligned with your values, you will not stick to it. It's like saying spinach is healthy, and you should eat it, but if you don't like it, you won't eat it. You should do it, but you won't.

Intentional spending means spending money with a purpose. When you slow down and gain an appreciation of how money helps you live, you will be more purposeful in your spending. When you spend money, you'll understand why you're spending that money, and how it fits into your overall picture.

Why Mindful and Intentional Spending Matters

Becoming mindful and intentional in your spending helps increase your net worth. You cannot expect to build wealth if you're spending more money than you're making. No matter how much you save, you'll continue to acquire debt, and the interest from that debt will keep you at a negative net worth. That's why you had to begin by examining your income and expenses and how they relate to one another.

Our society has made it much easier for you to be a mindless and unintentional consumer. Let's look back at how money exchange has evolved over time.

In 1990, you would go to the retail store to buy a product and pay cash for it. If the amount was $7.79, you gave the cashier the exact amount using paper money and coins or paid with all paper money and the change was returned to you.

Fast-forward a few years, and that same $7.79 purchase was paid for with a check. The check was completed with the date, the retail store's name, the amount of the purchase written both numerically and spelled out, then signed by you. It took three or four days for money to be withdrawn from your account.

Fast-forward several more years, and checks lost significant market share to "plastic." This typically meant debit cards, which drew money directly from your account. Or even more "awesome," you could make the purchase with a credit card and not even pay the $7.79 for this product for an entire month! These innovations made it easier and faster to just swipe a card to make a purchase. For a while, you had to sign the receipt to endorse the purchase, which slowed it down somewhat. Over the span of time, however, that practice became obsolete in most places too.

I remember the day I got a Discover card that was attached to my car key ring. I felt pretty cool! Not only that, but I also saved time in the checkout line because I did not have to dig in my purse and then wallet searching for my credit card. I already had my car keys in hand ready to leave, so my payment source was handy. One swipe and I was out the door.

After this, cashless money exchanges and digital wallets became available. People use Venmo and PayPal or tap their phone on a screen to complete a transaction. It's never been easier to spend money mindfully and unintentionally.

Here's a funny story:

My niece is forty-five years old, and her three cousins are younger than she is by ten years or so. She was collecting money from them to buy flowers for their uncle's funeral. No one had checks to pay her, and she did not have Venmo, so it was a challenge for them to exchange money.

With one cousin living at a distance, paying cash was not an option unless it was sent through the mail. My niece said that she felt like a dinosaur in her old-fashioned ways of trying to transact with the younger generation!

Today, e-commerce has emerged. Online marketplaces like Amazon allow you to shop in the comfort of your home at any hour of the day. You simply place items in an online shopping cart, click purchase, and the product shows up at your front door within a day or two. You can even buy it with one click. Talk about convenience! Talk about mindless.

In 1990, I knew exactly how much I was paying for a product by using cash. In the current decade, it's all about the swipe of a card or smartwatch or the push of buttons on a cell phone to make a payment. This enables you to make quick, mindless purchase decisions.

Research shows you are the most aware of your spending when using cash, followed by writing checks, then debit or credit cards, and least aware with linked accounts used for e-commerce retailers. That is not an accident. Consumers must increase spending awareness and focus on mindful, intentional spending.

[Use the Companion Guide to reflect on your payment methods. Has your payment method caused you to be a mindless spender?]

In this chapter, you're going to reclaim the art of becoming a mindful and intentional spender. To do that, you're going to need to think about the consumer decision-making process, understand it inside and out, and learn how to leverage it for more intentionality. This process not only works with finances but can be modified to help you work through any decision you are trying to make at the time.

Then, I will cover the SAVE approach for circumventing mindless spending. Following this, emotional spending triggers will be discussed along with strategies on how to replace them. Finally, I'll share easy ways to spend less without it hurting, so you can lower your expenses even further. This will make it much easier to have an income vs. expenses surplus and segue nicely into the chapter about making more money.

First is the consumer decision-making process.

Understand the Consumer Decision-Making Process

Every purchase you make follows this general framework, from buying a candy bar to buying a house. However, the process might reshuffle, merge, or skip some of the steps. Still, this process is repeated for everything you buy—but you don't always see it. You need to become aware of the universal buying process, so you can become a more mindful and intentional spender. Let's take a look at it through the lens of buying a car.

1. Problem Recognition

Every single purchase you make solves a problem of some kind (unless it is an emotional purchase of an unnecessary want). The problem could be hunger, or shelter, or any number of issues that arise. When you buy a car, the problem is generally that you need reliable transportation to get you to your job as well as all the activities of life. The awareness could come through a previous vehicle breaking down or moving to a place where you can't rely on public transportation any longer, etc. Regardless, now you have a problem to solve.

2. Information Search

Next, list all possible options. In the case of transportation, you might take a look at public transportation, the option to buy a used car, or the option to buy a brand-new car. You look for all the ways to solve the problem you have. Sometimes in this stage, you may determine a way to solve the problem that doesn't require a purchase, such as using the bicycle you have in your garage for a time. In other instances, you will decide that you want to move forward with a purchase of some kind.

3. Evaluating the Alternatives

Here, you compare and contrast all the options available to you. Not only do you decide on which category of item to buy, but you also compare between items within that category. So you may evaluate that you want the flexibility that having a car offers over public transportation, then decide that you want to save some money (or avoid debt) by purchasing a used car rather than a new car. From there, you repeat the cycle of gathering information about the types of cars to purchase and evaluating the results until you arrive at a decision.

4. Making the Purchase

For most products you buy, there is more than one way to complete the purchase. You might find a way to get the product through online shopping, or you might drive to a specific boutique for it. You could even go to a larger marketplace like a mall and evaluate more options from there. In terms of buying a used car, this typically means shopping online at dealerships and digital marketplaces or visiting dealerships in person. At the end of this phase, you trade your money for the item.

5. Post Purchase Evaluation

I consider this as one of the most important steps in the process, yet it is often overlooked. Evaluating the purchase after you make it is where you decide whether the product was worth the cost. A mindful and intentional spender sets aside time and space to think about and evaluate their purchases after they make them. You will be satisfied, not satisfied and return the item, or learn from your buying mistake so you can adjust your future behavior.

Post-purchase evaluation also helps you eliminate future decisions. If you find a product that you like, and it performs to your satisfaction, you can make repeat purchases of that same product or brand.

No matter what you buy, you follow this general process. However, trouble can arise when you skip steps. For example, some people might encounter the problem of transportation and immediately think, "New car," without taking the time to gather information and evaluate all the potential solutions to their problem. Skipping steps like this could hurt your overall financial picture and reinforce habits of mindless spending.

When you make purchases, especially large ones, make sure that you thoroughly complete every step of the process, and take your time at each phase. This doesn't mean that you need to take two weeks to decide whether to purchase a candy bar, but it does mean that your mindfulness and intentionality increase with the higher risk purchases that cost more and impact your financial picture.

[Use the Companion Guide to practice working through these steps.]

Think SAVE to Battle Mindless Spending

Now that you understand the consumer decision-making process, you can include the SAVE approach to promote mindful and intentional spending. This approach leverages the consumer decision-making process and has built-in mechanisms to ensure that your spending aligns with your financial goals. It's also an easy-to-remember acronym.

S Is for STOP

When you feel the urge to make a purchase, stop and wait. For nearly anything you buy, you don't have to complete the transaction immediately, or even that day. The higher the risk of the purchase, the more time should be spent in the consumer decision-making process. For example, if you're thinking about buying a lower risk item, say $20, you can stop and wait for an hour or two to determine whether it is something you truly need. If it's something bigger, like a vehicle, you might wait several days before committing.

A Is for Analyze

Remember when I talked about how many shampoos you could buy at the store? It's both a blessing and a curse that you have so many options available to select from in this day and age. During your waiting period, analyze the various options available to you. Higher risk items will require more time to analyze. For nearly anything you want to purchase, there will likely be a less expensive alternative or a way to get your problem solved that requires less or even no money.

V Is for Verify

At the end of your waiting process, make the decision again. Do you really want to make this purchase, or was it just a momentary urge? This is also a space to ask yourself whether you really need this product in your life, and whether it will positively impact you ten years from now. Regardless of your final decision, you know that you've been mindful and intentional about the process, and you should have peace about the purchase.

E Is for Execute

In the end, you either buy or you don't buy. Sometimes you'll find that you want a less expensive alternative, or that you didn't really want the product at all. Or you still want it, but you see that it doesn't fit with your financial plan. Other times, you'll move forward with the purchase, knowing that you went through a mindful process to ensure that it's the solution you want for your problem.

This is the framework you need to combat emotional spending. That said, emotional spending is powerful. Next are some additional strategies to overcome it.

Overcome Emotional Spending

Several years ago, my husband and I had a garage sale. A neighbor made several trips to our sale carrying her "finds" back to her house and then returning to spend more. She purchased one item too large for her to carry alone, so my husband and I offered to help. She opened her garage door, and it was full—and I mean *full*—from wall to wall and floor to ceiling of stuff.

She seriously could've opened her garage door and had a rummage sale herself, yet she was still adding to her own clutter. As a seller, I was delighted to get rid of my stuff, but it made me uneasy that she was on the other end buying stuff that she didn't need, as a result of emotional spending.

My neighbor did not know that she was an emotional spender, but as soon as that garage door opened, I knew that there was a serious problem. Last chapter, I went over some of the signs that you may be an emotional spender. If those resonated with you, this section will give you some strategies for addressing emotional spending. Even if you don't identify as an emotional spender, these strategies can help you become more mindful and intentional.

1. Identify Your Emotional Spending Triggers

Some people make emotional purchases when they feel sad or lonely. Others do it as a way to celebrate. When you make purchases, begin asking yourself these questions:

    a. How did I feel prior to the purchase? What made me feel that way?

    b. How did I feel during the purchase?

    c. How did I feel after purchasing?

This will help you identify the emotions and situations that lead to unnecessary spending. Asking yourself these questions for your purchases will begin to show you the triggers.

2. Review Your Values, Vision, and Goals

The reason that emotional spending busts your budget is because it causes you to make purchases unaligned with your values, vision, and goals. So, to begin overcoming emotional spending, you must consistently refresh yourself on what you're doing and why. This is why you put your goals in a place where you can see them every day; it keeps the goal top-of-mind and affects the decisions that you make. Reminding yourself of your financial vision will provide you with motivation to make a different choice in the moment.

3. Navigate Difficult Emotions

When an emotional spending trigger happens, there is a twofold process for overcoming emotional spending. First, you must learn how to deal with the emotion itself, whatever it is. Half the battle here is identifying the emotion in the first place. Perhaps you make emotional purchases whenever you feel stressed, and long work days trigger that stress in you. If that's the case, acknowledge the emotion you're feeling in the moment. Speak it aloud or write it down. Instead of coping with the emotion by making a purchase, you're confronting it directly.

4. Use Replacement Behaviors to Avoid Emotional Spending

It's nearly impossible to get rid of an unhelpful habit without replacing it with something else. Simply telling yourself, "I'm going to stop emotional spending" without deciding to do something different in the moment will probably not get you very far. Instead, you need to commit to replacement behaviors on the front end that help you work through the emotion. Depending on the trigger, this could look different. Perhaps if you are stressed, you can identify the trigger and go on a walk outside to dissipate some of the negative emotions. Or you can talk through your situation with a loved one.

No matter the trigger, simply sitting there and trying not to make an emotional purchase will be difficult. Come up with a list of replacement behaviors that don't cost money and have them at the ready for when the trigger comes. Over time, it will reprogram your automatic response to the trigger, and you'll be left with a positive habit.

When you understand the consumer decision-making process and overcome emotional spending, it causes you to spend less. This leads to lower expenses, making it easier to increase your net worth. However, there are times when you simply have to make a purchase. There's no way to entirely eliminate expenses from your life. But there are ways to spend less without being too hard on yourself.

[Use the Companion Guide to evaluate your emotional spending habits.]

Spend Less without It Hurting

You need to improve your income vs. expenses to increase your surplus. This will enable you to direct your surplus into areas that help you pay off debt and increase your net worth through investments. The next chapter will discuss ways to make more money. Before that, I want to discuss strategies that help you spend less without too much sacrifice.

1. Focus On Cost per Serving

Instead of making purchasing decisions based on the sticker price, look at the cost per serving. Many retail stores include this information on the store shelf, but if not, it typically requires a simple math calculation on your phone. Look for options that are lower price-per-serving, and also, make sure that serving serves you well! For example, I use a paper towel brand that costs more according to the sticker—but I use far less of it due to how absorbent the sheets are. So, overall, my cost is lower for the amount I use.

2. Buy Reasonable Quality

You don't have to begin making every purchase a low-quality, huge quantity bulk buy. For one, you may not have enough room in your pantry or house for those kinds of purchases. Instead, focus on reasonable quality, a happy medium between quantity and quality. For nearly any purchase, there is a slightly lower quality alternative for a decently lower price. When seeking to spend less without it hurting, consider downgrading these common purchases by just one tier of acceptable quality, and see how much it saves you.

3. Distinguish between Needs and Wants

This is where the work that you did in chapter 5 on expenses will pay off. There are many items you purchase because you want them, but not necessarily because you need them. Additionally, you have a multitude of products that you buy but don't really use. When you spend money on everything you need and begin to leave off things that you merely want, it won't feel like too large of a sacrifice.

4. Take Advantage of Sales and Coupons

Buy products when they are in season (fruits and vegetables) or when they go on sale (at the end of the year or after holidays). Don't buy an item just because it's on sale, or you have a coupon for it. Only buy it if you need it and it fits in your monthly budget.

5. Comparison Shop

Compare price and quality at three or more sources for the product you want to buy. Remember the consumer decision-making process states that your purchase is attempting to solve a problem. There's always more than one way to solve this problem. Comparison shopping can also help you negotiate price matching at the store of your choice. Some big-box retailers will price match and meet any competitor's price.

6. Only Make Purchases within Your Plan

Making a precommitment is a powerful psychological tool. Oftentimes, you make unnecessary purchases because you haven't committed not to. So, when you see an item you want, or an emotional spending trigger occurs, you have an internal debate with the temptation to buy it. If you've already decided, that debate never starts. To make this commitment, frequently review your plan.

7. Eat Out Less

When people begin learning finances from me and follow the exercises I give them, it often astounds them how much they spend eating out. Therefore, this is one of the best ways to get a quick boost to your income vs. expenses. Commit at the beginning of the month to how many times you will eat out and make a budget for those meals. Then, plan ahead for your other meals at home and shop at the grocery store accordingly.

Visit my website (Anchord.money) to access the *Surefire Approach to Slash Your Spending*, which includes over one thousand tips on reducing spending in every product category – for FREE. While you likely won't implement them all, simply doing five to ten of them will help your financial situation. Some are tips you may have never even thought of, so it's just a matter of making a slight change for increased savings.

Chapter Summary

You may wonder why I spend so much time talking about emotional spending, but remember, 90 percent emotions and 10 percent logic are used when spending. I do it, you do it, everyone does it. Even if you don't think that you are an emotional spender, it happens more than you think. Reducing your expenses is an important part of mindful and intentional money management. It's often the first step when it comes to executing a personal process for financial success. To reduce expenses, become a mindful and intentional spender and take the time to understand and incorporate the consumer decision-making process, the SAVE method, and strategies for overcoming emotional spending and spending less (without it hurting).

 ## KEY TAKEAWAYS

- Mindful and intentional spending is based on your individual lifestyle and consciously spending money with the purpose of helping increase your net worth.
- Use the consumer decision-making process, along with the SAVE approach, to help you to become a mindful and intentional consumer.
- Identifying emotional spending triggers and replacing them with behaviors that don't cost money will reduce your spending.
- Use simple cost-saving strategies to spend less money without it hurting.

CHAPTER 11:

Making More Money

Making more money is the second half of the equation when it comes to improving your income vs. expenses. The last chapter listed strategies for reducing expenses. This chapter will further discuss ways to increase income than those included in chapter 4. When you combine these strategies, it will help you move from a deficit to a surplus in your monthly budget. This is absolutely necessary if you want to pay off debt and increase your net worth.

In the last two chapters, you learned how to set yourself up for success. This involved building a mind map for your finances and strategies to combat emotional spending. The content in this chapter and the previous one will form the basis of your plan for personal financial success. The final chapter is about executing that plan, building muscle memory to make your success automatic. After this, your journey through this book will be over, but

I will leave you with plenty of options to make sure that you are not alone when you close the book.

When someone wants to improve their income vs. expenses picture, they often solely look at their income and avoid looking at expenses, thinking that they can outearn out-of-control spending. Budget leaks and mindless spending will outpace any attempts to earn more money. If that's your strategy, every pay raise or income increase will cause you to spend even more money. So that mindset must be taken care of first. I urge you to make sure you've implemented the strategies to become a mindful and intentional spender; otherwise, you run the risk of burning yourself out by trying to make more money with a leaking budget.

With that said, there are multiple paths to take when it comes to making more money. The specific strategies you use will depend on your goals, needs, and life stage. I encourage you to revisit the timeline of your goals as you plan your methods for making more money. It will often take longer than you think to achieve milestones in the short term, but with deliberate planning and execution, you will go further than you thought over the long term. Long story short, make sure you set goals that work in your world, and take your time and energy into account.

For example, a single person with no children may be able to implement more of these strategies than someone who is married with four children involved in sports, while both were working in established careers. Neither of these positions is better than the other, but they simply affect which strategies the individual will go to first.

Straight Talk: Hard Work

Let's get serious for a minute. Although I've talked about taking your family situation and energy into account, that's not an excuse to do nothing. If you want to fix your financial situation, it will typically take a temporary season of hard work and sacrifice. This looks like reducing unnecessary expenses and working harder for months or even years. To get to our financial goals, there were years when my husband and I both worked multiple jobs and spent very little beyond the bare necessities. It was difficult, but it was necessary and now worth it. Nothing beats the feeling you get when you pay off all your debts (including the house) and see your net worth begin to increase.

Diversification Is Powerful

Here's another note before going into specific strategies. Financial experts often talk about diversifying your portfolio when it comes to investments. This means investing in multiple different areas, using multiple kinds of investments. The reason they do this is because it creates a safer and more stable investment portfolio over time.

A diversified portfolio is more likely to increase over time. If one stock or fund decreases, it doesn't have as much of an effect when it's only one stock of many. Diversification is also powerful for your income. That's why you may want to consider setting up multiple streams of income, especially during a phase of aggressively paying off debt. If one stream of income gets smaller or dries up, it won't harm your financial picture. Plus, during different seasons, different streams will increase to compensate.

There is no "right" number of streams of income but having at least three or four will help you get to an income vs. expenses surplus quickly and achieve your financial goals. These streams of income could include jobs, side hustles, real estate investments, short-term investments, royalties from media you produce, using a property as an Airbnb or Vrbo, and so much more.

The remainder of the chapter will cover ways to increase your income. Be sure to carefully research options that are safe and where you can earn the most money for your time. Choose the ones that fit your circumstances and begin diversifying your income streams.

18 Ways to Make More Money

I will divide methods for increasing your income into five primary categories. Each of them may fit your goals and preferences, depending on your stage of life. You can make more money through your primary job, an additional job, side hustles, passive income, and selling stuff. This is not a comprehensive list, but it does offer plenty of ideas for you to get started and covers the most common methods.

A. Earning More through Your Job

Many people can earn additional income through their primary job. It requires learning additional skills or investing additional time, but it has the benefit of not requiring an extra commute or context.

1. Get Promoted

If you're serious about increasing your income, you might find out how to get promoted at your current job. This could mean going from a member of your department to a manager of that department or a similar one. Depending on your job, getting promoted may be a matter of asking your manager what you need to do and doing it. It could also involve learning additional skills or acquiring a certification.

2. Get a Raise

This can often happen more quickly than a promotion, though it can happen through similar means. Ask your manager what they want to see from you in order to get a raise, and do it. Many jobs have built-in performance reviews throughout the year when raises are on the table, so getting a raise could be as simple as bringing your best effort to work and asking for one.

3. Work Overtime/Extra Shifts

Many jobs have options for overtime, and not everyone takes them. If you find yourself in a season where you need to make additional money, take as much overtime and extra shifts as you can handle. Additionally, if you have a work environment where people trade shifts or need coverage for time off, accept those shifts as well. Overtime also comes with an increased hourly rate for your efforts.

4. Join a Committee or Board

Some workplaces have additional committees and boards that meet outside traditional work hours. You could see what it takes to join one and whether it comes with additional pay. Plus, many corporations and nonprofits need board members. Depending on your work experience, you could join a board and take part in the meetings.

B. Earning More through an Additional Job

Another main way to earn more money is through an additional job. If you're already working full-time, this often means working a job that takes place in the evenings and weekends, or on a seasonal basis.

1. Pick Up a Second Job

One option could be to pick up a new job in the service sector, preferably one that pays tips. As I mentioned earlier, one of my daughters had a season where she worked a job that offered tips in addition to her day job, so she could have a surplus in her income vs. expenses. Your second job could be relatively unskilled or relate to skills you have but aren't using in your primary job.

2. Go Back to School/Learn a Trade

You could also use the evenings and weekends to attend classes or learn a trade. This could cost money on the front end unless you diligently acquire scholarships or save money for the tuition. It's a longer-term strategy, but it could lead to you getting a new primary job that pays more than your current one. Check with your employer about tuition recovery options where they will pay all or a part of your tuition.

C. Earning More through Side Hustles

Besides formal employment, there are an increasing number of side hustles available in the modern age. It's never been easier to earn money through a variety of sources, and some of them don't even require you to leave your house.

1. Become a Freelancer

There are plenty of freelance jobs available online depending on your skills. Additionally, some of them hardly require any skill or training. Here is a brief list of potential freelance jobs:

- Writing, editing, and proofreading
- Transcribing audio into subtitles or transcripts
- Art and graphic design
- Bookkeeping and accounting
- Customer service
- Sales
- Virtual assistance

There are many online job boards to apply these (and other) freelance trades.

2. Sell Art and Crafts

If you have artistic, photographic, or crafting talent, you could turn that into increased income. There are websites that pay photographers for the licensing on their stock photos. You can also sell art designs and crafts online through marketplaces.

3. Drive People and Deliver Things

If you have a reliable car, you can spend evenings and weekends using it to make money. This could come in the form of ridesharing, grocery delivery, laundry services, cleaning, or food and drink orders. Look for options in your community, as people are always seeking services to support their active lifestyles. Again, this doesn't have to be permanent, and always consider the safety of these jobs.

4. Teach and Coach

You could coach a sport or direct/chaperone extracurricular activities for schools in your areas, or even teach a course in an area of your expertise at a community college. If you know more than one language, you could teach English or your additional language online or in person. There are even services to teach English as a second language online. Lastly, you could tutor students at a school or college in a subject area you have expertise in.

5. Help People Gather Data

There are also plenty of organizations that pay people to help gather data. This could come in the form of using and testing apps or answering surveys. Some sites will even pay people to be a mystery shopper at a store and answer questions about their experience. Finally, you can see whether the colleges and universities in your area need any participants in research studies.

D. Earning More through Passive Income

One of the most efficient ways to earn money is to make your money work for you, or to set up income streams that pay you automatically. Some of these require a decent amount of time and effort on the front end, but less in the long run.

1. Make Investments

Investments are one of the most straightforward ways to earn passive income. These can come in the form of dividends from investments in the stock market or bonds, but also assets like real estate. Again, don't enter the real estate market without conducting an extensive amount of research.

2. Sell Assets Online

This strategy involves creating learning materials and downloadable documents online and selling them to those who want to learn. If you have an area of expertise, you could create an online course and sell it, getting paid by the download.

3. Monetize Entertainment

If you have a knack for writing, creating video content, or entertaining people live, you can use it to make money. It often takes dedication to create a following, but you could monetize a blog through advertising, monetize videos, or even stream yourself playing games or talking to people on social media.

E. Earning More through Selling Stuff

This is something that was touched on in previous chapters, but it's worthwhile for rounding out the list. I will also offer a couple of additional ideas that I haven't mentioned before. Selling items is a great way to increase your income, and almost everyone can benefit from it.

1. Downgrade/Downsize Items

Depending on your stage of life, you may be able to make a great deal of money from downsizing or downgrading high-value possessions. For example, if you have a large house, but your children have moved out, and you're not using all the space, you could consider selling the house and moving into something smaller. Or, if you have a newer model of car, you could sell it and go for a less expensive model.

2. Sell Unnecessary Items

This includes furniture you don't sit on, appliances you don't use, electronics you haven't turned on in years, exercise equipment, and more. Additionally, you may have some collector's items tucked away that have appreciated in value. Almost everyone has items to sell that they don't really use—and after your net worth increases, you can buy almost anything back.

3. Sell Books and Textbooks

Selling books is a related idea that I haven't shared yet: You can trade in your old textbooks and other books online or at your school bookstore. Many people have books they don't read or have already read lying around their house. Additionally, some people have books they had to buy for college and now have no need for. Selling or trading them in can boost your income.

4. Sell Other People's Stuff

You can find items that people are giving away for free as you drive around, or on websites. If you can get something for free and then turn around and sell it for money, it will boost your income. Depending on how crafty you are, you could acquire old furniture that people are giving away, fix it up, and flip it.

Set SMARTER Income Goals

Remember, your goals need to work in your world. That isn't to say you can't be aggressive or work really hard for a short season of time, but you also need to be realistic. For example, if you have a full-time job, a spouse, and several children, you probably can't do everything on this list. However, regardless of your situation, there's always something you can do.

So develop a custom plan for yourself. The best way to do this is through setting a SMARTER goal for increasing your income. Setting SMARTER goals was covered in chapter 3, but as a brief refresher, your income boosting goal should be

- Specific
- Measurable
- Achievable
- Relevant
- Time-Bound
- Exciting
- Recorded

For example, you could say, "For the next six months, I will increase my income by $500 each month, so I can pay off the credit card and enjoy the relief that brings. I will do so by picking up a job at the local coffee shop on Saturdays and Sundays and following my monthly budget plan." Notice how that goal fulfills all the criteria? Your goal should do the same.

A final note: This isn't forever. I like to call it "getting over the hump." Six months of reducing your expenses and increasing your income might seem like a long time, but if that's what it takes to get debt paid off, then it isn't that big of a deal in the long run. It may require discomfort for a temporary period of time, but it will lead to greater calm in your finances over the long term. Even if you must make tough choices for a short period of time, it'll be worth it when your credit card balance is $0, or you can afford the down payment on your first home.

[Use the Companion Guide to determine which strategies to increase income may work for you.]

At this point, you've learned and planned a personal process for financial success. Fixing your DTI is a crucial step in reaching your financial goals and increasing your net worth. Now, all that remains is to make your future success automatic (and less painful).

Chapter Summary

Making more money is the second part of getting to a surplus in your income vs. expenses. Once you have your expenses reduced and you are practicing mindful and intentional spending, strategize the ways you can increase your income for a temporary season. I listed eighteen ways to make more money in five different categories for you to implement depending on your life stage and goal. You can choose the ones that work for you and set a SMARTER goal for this temporary season of making more money.

 | **KEY TAKEAWAYS**

- Your income can't outpace out-of-control spending.
- Having multiple streams of income helps you diversify income sources. This can be done through your current job, an additional job, side hustles, passive income, and selling stuff.
- Develop a custom plan for increasing your income. How much do you need to increase your income by each month? For how long?
- Using those answers (and pointing back to your values), develop a SMARTER goal for your income.
- Commit to tough choices and a sacrifice of energy and time. It will be worth it!

CHAPTER 12:

Building Muscle Memory to Make Your Future Success Automatic (and Less Painful)

Your journey through this book is almost over, but your new financial journey is just beginning. So far, you've learned where you're going and where you're at, and you've also learned and planned a personal process for financial success. Now, all that remains is to make that process automatic and execute.

After your time in these pages is done, I want to remind you that you're not alone. That's not just an empty phrase; I will be sharing valuable resources for you to continue the journey and become part of a community committed to mindful and intentional money. Before you finish this book, though, I want to help you build what I call "money muscle memory" so you can make your money management much easier.

As you learn how to do anything new with your body, like riding a bike, swimming, or even pitching a baseball, it will hurt. Your muscles will protest after you're done with your first training session. If you decide to start working out at the gym, you might wake up the next day feeling all kinds of sore. Over time, though, you get used to it. The same goes for a financial journey, moving from chaos to calm. It may feel uncomfortable at first, but eventually it will become habitual.

Also, when you learn how to bike, swim, or pitch, it will feel uncoordinated and disjointed at first. As you teach your muscles the movements, there will be stumbles, falls, and curveballs that end up in the dirt. But if you don't give up, eventually these skills become unforgettable. Likewise, as you apply these money lessons in the real world, it will begin to feel like second nature. Your life will get even easier as it gets more and more automatic.

This works the same as it does in all walks of life. Take sports for instance and a friend of mine who we'll call Paul for the purposes of this story. Paul coaches his two kids in sports—his son in basketball and his daughter in softball. He's been coaching them since they were very young. If you have never had the experience of coaching kids in sports, the secret, at least according to Paul, is to get the kids to stop thinking about what they're doing—to teach them a few simple ideas in a way that sounds natural and then encourage them to take their minds out of what they're doing and just let their bodies work.

"When my son was younger, it didn't matter how many defensive drills we practiced, when the games started, everyone acted as if it was their first time on a court. Every team was like that. They'd practice drills. They'd learn spacing and strategies. And then, when the games started, it was essentially ten kids running into each other."

After two games, Paul decided to do something different. In practice, he held a scrimmage and the only instruction he gave the kids was to lift one hand in the air when the person they were guarding was shooting the ball, as if they were trying to get their teacher's attention. As the scrimmage progressed, he resisted the urge to yell out any other directions, just "hand in the air" whenever he saw someone about to shoot.

At first, it was messy. Some kids didn't get it right away. Others almost slapped the kid they were guarding in the face. But by the end of the practice, the kids got it. Every time someone was about to shoot, the defender's hand would go straight in the air.

Paul knew that, at that age, all it would take to rattle the offensive player enough to miss or pull the ball back down and shoot was one hand in the air.

But would it translate to a game? You guessed it. By taking out the complications of defense and only encouraging his kids to "raise their hand like they were trying to get their teacher's attention" when the player they were guarding was about to shoot, Paul created an almost reflexive reaction in those kids to simply raise their hand when they saw the person they were guarding beginning to lift the ball up to shoot.

Instantly, his team became one of the best defensive groups in the league, not by implementing some complex defensive strategy but by keeping it simple and creating muscle memory so nobody had to think about what their feet were doing or how much space they were creating. All they needed to do was raise their hand.

Paul used that same concept, keeping it simple and building muscle memory to teach the kids how to protect the ball after they get a rebound ("Hug the ball like it's a long lost relative until all the other players run away so they don't steal the ball from you") and countering when the other team sets up a pick play where one offensive player blocks the path of a defender so the offensive player the defender was guarding can get a free shot ("When they pick, we switch").

Paul focused one or more entire practices on one drill until it became second nature (read: muscle memory) to the young kids. Today, more than five years later, Paul still coaches his son's basketball team, and you can tell which kids he coached in previous years because they all *still* have the same instinctive reaction when their opponents get ready to shoot, when they get a rebound, when the other team sets a pick, and other common basketball situations. Even playing on other teams in the league, the boys who have been coached by Paul in the past *still* instinctively raise one hand when the person they are defending starts to raise the ball to shoot, give the basketball a full bear hug when they get a rebound, and "switch" with another teammate on defense when the offense sets a "pick" on one defender. Years later. Without even thinking.

That's muscle memory.

And it makes doing the work so much easier.

It makes doing the things that make you succeed happen virtually automatically.

Financial Muscle Memory

In this chapter, you're going to learn what financial muscle memory means, learn how to break and replace habits and vices, and learn how to apply financial automations. This will make it so you don't have to be in a constant decision-making mode that leads to fatigue and burnout. When that happens, you get overwhelmed and often fall back into your former spending patterns.

Let me go back to the shampoo aisle analogy where I talked about having hundreds of options available to you. Today, you probably don't have to think much when you go to that aisle. You have a go-to brand and product for shampoo that you buy, and maybe even a backup option if it's out of stock. For some items, you can walk through a store and find exactly what you need without thought, without having to expend much energy.

That's essentially what you're going to learn to do here. This will make finances in general simpler for you. There are certain decisions you only have to make once, and then never really have to think about again. Through the post evaluation step in the consumer decision-making process, you have determined a product that best works for you so you can make repeat purchases. However, that does not mean that your automatic purchases should not be periodically evaluated to make sure that another product performs as well for less money.

It takes some groundwork at the beginning. Going through your finances for the first time is like going to the shampoo aisle for the first time. You might have to read and study a ton before making a decision and moving forward. Eventually, though, you have a plan that works in the real world without it consuming your life.

How to Grow Your Financial Confidence with Marissa Iles

Marissa Iles grew up with a single mother, who worked hard to provide for her kids and support them. Growing up, Marissa would hear horror stories about how easily life could get out of hand for people in that vulnerable position.

Going into college, she was unsure of how to secure her own financial stability. She appreciated how much her own mother had sacrificed to raise her, but she didn't know how to build a solid financial future for herself. This led to a lack of confidence.

What is confidence? Where does it come from?

Many people mistake confidence for bravado. Confidence isn't pretending to be more qualified than you currently are. It doesn't come from bravery or courage. In reality, confidence comes from skill and competence. When you know you can face the challenges in front of you because you have the right tools in your hands, you automatically gain confidence.

So, to gain financial confidence, you need the right tools to build your skill and competence. When you employ the tools in this book to start moving toward positive and growing net worth, and you understand how to make and stick to a budget, you begin to have confidence.

During her time as my student, Marissa learned how to be mindful and intentional with her money. Not only did she get the right tools for her personal finances, but she also learned how to educate others. This led to a career in student finance, turning around and helping college students learn how to become mindful and intentional with their own money. In no time, she climbed the ladder and enjoyed several managerial positions. Now, she runs a business in event and wedding planning while also managing projects for trade shows.

Because Marissa got ahead of the game as a student, she is equipped to handle finances for herself and for her business. In the same way, when you learn and apply the techniques I've taught you, you'll begin to feel more financial confidence.

Make Your Plan Work in the Real World

It's good to have lofty financial goals, but your plan won't serve you unless every step along the way is realistic and achievable. That's why when you set a long-term financial goal in chapter 3, you also set intermediate- and short-term goals. This way, you can connect what you do every day, week, and month to reach your desired destination over the span of decades and see achievements along the way. There are two additional ways to make your plan work better in the real world:

1. Make things work without you having to think about them. This is where muscle memory comes into play. Muscle memory is closely related to your habits. The less you must think, the more automatically you behave, the more likely your plan is to come to reality.

2. Take decisions off your plate. This involves setting up automations. Decision fatigue is a real thing, especially in the age of options. Automations will help you make fewer decisions, reserving emotional energy for the decisions that matter most, and giving you more back over all. This will also make your plan for financial success more likely to be achieved.

With those two concepts in mind, let's look at muscle memory and then automations:

What Is Muscle Memory?

Imagine it's a Tuesday night, and you just got off work at six o'clock. In many areas, it's considered Taco Tuesday—a popular promotional phrase started in 1982 by a chain called Taco John's. Your stomach is already rumbling, and you're looking forward to supper. However, there's just one little problem: nothing is prepared. In this situation, you have a few options. This is a perfect "storm" and sets you up for a mindless spending situation: you just get off work, it's Taco Tuesday, you're starving, and there's nothing at home to eat (or so you think).

Your option is to eat out, or at least get takeout. Or you might have someone deliver some food to your door. If you have a spouse, you might have to have the "'What do you want to eat?' 'I don't know, what do you want to eat?'" conversation. All this costs time, money, and emotional energy. By this time, you are not only hungry but now "hangry"—hungry and angry!

Now, imagine it's that same hungry Tuesday night, but you have a plan in place. You know that on Tuesday, you fix tacos because, after all, it's Taco Tuesday. So you've already prepared everything on Sunday and put it in the fridge. You're going to drive home, heat it up, and enjoy a fine meal. This situation requires no additional thinking, conversation, or decisions. Plus, it will save you money!

That example shows the power of habits and muscle memory, and it's also a specific tactic you can use to save yourself time and money.

Decision Fatigue

Decision fatigue is the exhaustion that comes from making too many choices. We all have a limited amount of time and energy every day. This time and energy gets debited every time you make a decision. When you constantly must make decisions, you often get drawn to the easiest decision, taking the path of least resistance. So the Tuesday night example turns into "let's just get tacos," because it's an easy decision to make. Plus, in an age where companies can save your address, favorite order, and card number on their website, it gets that much easier (and more expensive for you).

Another option, when you fire up the grill to cook something like chicken, throw on some hamburgers and hot dogs. These can then be refrigerated and eaten throughout the week, again reducing decisions and the temptation to eat out. Just warm up the leftovers, add a side dish or two, and you have a nice meal.

Predeciding and precommitting are the counter to decision fatigue. In the supper analogy, it means planning out the week of meals, buying and cooking in bulk, and freezing or refrigerating the food. It ultimately saves time, energy, and money, but it requires work on the front end. Therefore, it's not the path of least resistance—at least at first. Making decisions about your finances ahead of time, and making them automatic, combats decision fatigue.

Now that you understand the main concepts, you need to get practical. The first step to putting muscle memory and automations into place is breaking and replacing bad habits.

Break and Replace Habits

I mentioned during the section on emotional spending triggers that it is difficult to stop a bad habit. You can't break a habit unless you replace it with something else, something better for you. Take, for example, the analogy of going to the same coffee shop each morning and buying an expensive beverage. This habit could cost you hundreds of dollars every month after all is said and done. However, simply telling yourself to stop likely won't work. You'll still want caffeine, and the taste, and the sense of routine as you prepare for your workday.

First, you need to break and replace the habit. Buy a nice coffee pot for your home and select your favorite coffee varieties. A travel mug will be useful to take your coffee on the go. If you are still tempted to stop, you could take a different route to work that doesn't pass by that coffee shop. Think about the time saved not sitting in the coffee line to place your order. That's a bonus to your changed behavior.

Take some time to consider the financial habits you have, and which ones you need to break and replace. A good way to do this is to view your expenses from the past month and see which ones recur. When you've identified a habit that you want to change, don't just break it, but replace it with something else.

Straight Talk: Vices

Many of the stereotypical "bad habits" people have are budget busters:

Tobacco products. While I would encourage you to stop because you're going to have health-related expenses later, not to mention how expensive it is to buy, you have to budget for it. Other financial planners may ignore this expense and simply advise you to stop using tobacco because it's a waste of money. That won't work because you are likely not going to quit because a financial planner tells you to. This will have to be done at a time when you are ready. However, can you reduce your tobacco usage to reduce the expense?

Alcohol. It costs a great deal when you purchase alcoholic beverages at restaurants and bars, and for some people, this is their social outing. You may consider how you can reduce what you spend on alcohol. For example, you could replace going out with friends to an expensive bar with inviting them over and having a couple of alcoholic beverages at home.

Gambling. I will just say that you may be on a slippery slope if you are not able to control this. Gambling is entertaining and fun, but dangerous. Most often, gamblers only think (and talk) about the times they won, and often think of excuses when they lose. Risk-takers and entrepreneurs are often susceptible to gambling because they may be more comfortable taking risks. Think about it, those big, beautiful casinos are not built based on payouts from winning.

Again, these three expenses can be budget busters, so you must include them in your financial plan if you choose to continue with them. Tracking your expenses for a month to see how much is spent on tobacco products, alcohol, and gambling might help you to either eliminate or reduce your spending in these areas. Again, that decision is up to you.

[Use the Companion Guide to develop strategies to make your plan work in the real world.]

Other financial planners will tell you to just stop. Stop smoking, Stop drinking. Stop gambling. Stop whatever vices are costing you money. Although that's not necessarily "bad" advice, I take a different approach, encouraging you to stop but at least making sure you're responsible about it if you can't, won't, or don't. At the very least, make sure what you spend on these vices is part of your overall financial plan, so your vices don't create bigger problems.

Automate Your Spending and Investing

The next step, after you've begun to replace bad habits with better ones, is to employ automations. This builds muscle memory into your finances and removes the need to make decisions.

1. Automate Your Spending

Many of your bills and expenses can be automated. Some of them even reward you for setting up an autopay because they know they won't have to bother you to collect a payment. Review your monthly expenses and see which payments can be automated. The results might surprise you. The more you automate, the less you need to think. You just need to account for the automatic payment in your monthly budget.

2. Review Your Subscriptions

That said, it's important to be mindful of everything you are automatically paying for. Subscriptions have a tendency to get out of hand if you don't pay careful attention. Subscriptions can include anything from streaming services, to storage, to downloads, etc. Set aside time once every few months to review everything you're subscribed to, and whether you're actually using it. If you're not using it at all, or only once a month or so, consider canceling it.

3. Automate Your Investments

In addition to your expenses, your investments can also be automated. I highly recommend this because it takes the decision and thought out of the equation. If you plan to invest in a retirement plan, 529 plan, or even an account to save up for a house or a car, automate it. Some workplaces automatically reserve a percentage of your paycheck into a retirement plan. Other automations can be set up with your bank or financial advisor.

4. Automate Your Debts

Going a step further, you can also automate your debt payments. This could mean an automatic withdrawal for the minimum amount on your mortgage, student loans, car payment, credit cards, and so on, but it goes beyond that. For some of them, you may be able to set up an automation to pay extra beyond the minimum. This will reduce the interest that gathers overall and enable you to get to positive net worth faster. For all your debt payments, determine whether you can make automatic payments above the minimum. Be sure that the additional payment goes directly toward the principle of the loan.

[Use the Companion Guide to determine which automations you can employ.]

Make Decisions Consistent with Your Goals

You don't have to live your life in a spreadsheet. A promise at the start of this book was that you don't need to be a math genius or accountant to figure out finances. It simply takes a bit of work on the front end. The more muscle memory you build, and the more automations you have, the less you'll have to worry about spreadsheets at all. It's just like learning to ride that bicycle. It may take some work and cause some pain on the front end, but eventually it becomes second nature. Eventually, you can go much further while expending less energy.

Money, Community, and Legacy with Jeanne Dau

Jeanne Dau is the founder of Dau Consulting. She's an entrepreneurial coach who specializes in helping people who want to impact their communities positively through new business ventures.

When we begin to move toward a positive and growing net worth, it often makes us think about how we can give back. How can we influence the community around us? What kind of legacy do we want to leave behind?

Jeanne works with plenty of movers and shakers in their communities who want to make a difference. She coaches current and aspiring small business owners who want to improve their surrounding community. The first place she advises them on is their personal finances.

Many people with an entrepreneurial mindset are risk-takers. This plays a role in their personal finances. Because most businesses require an investment on the front end, Jeanne often advises clients to build savings before launching their business. The better you do in your personal finances, the more you can give back to your community.

In previous decades, beginning a business often meant going to a bank for a loan. You had to present to the bank exactly why giving you a loan was a good investment for them and put up collateral. These days, the process can get short-circuited by online loans and crowdfunding, leading many entrepreneurs to dive headfirst into a business that they haven't thought through.

This plays into the larger issue of understanding your personality and how it influences your work and money. If you are a risk-taker who likes to think big, you need to surround yourself with people who think differently than you. Your business needs a strategy, and that strategy has to be adaptable. Additionally, it would be wise to find a mentor, a good person to bounce your financial ideas off of.

Jeanne uses the True Colors Personality Test in her consulting and for hiring within her own business. This test is based on the quadrants of the brain and their functions. Everyone prefers to live in one quadrant, and the quadrants can be broken down roughly as follows:

- Scientists and analysts who love numbers and dislike risk.

- Traditionalists and achievers who love schedules and dislike change.

- Social butterflies and community-minded people who love going along with their friends but don't always ask what they themselves want.

- Innovators and artists who come up with great ideas but often need to be reined in.

Jeanne notes that if you want to start a business, make sure that it aligns with your personality type, and bring in people who have different strengths than you. Plus, if you want to start a business, you'll probably need to increase your income and reduce debt for a season before launching. To do that, she recommends this system for finding a side gig:

1. Go through your day and take note of what you do by making a time log.

2. Write down which parts of the day made you happy. It might have been creating a budget, delivering a presentation, participating in a meeting, or moving a project along a timeline.

3. Ask yourself, how can I make money doing the part of the day that I loved?

Align your side gig with your personal happiness and passion, and you'll likely increase your income with it faster.

Now, as you move forward, keep making decisions consistent with your goals. When a financial decision arises, ask yourself the following questions:

- How do these choices fit into my overall financial goals?
- What are my values here?
- If this is a purchasing decision, will it matter in ten years? Will it get me closer to where I want to go or further away?
- Is there a way to automate this so I don't have to make the decision again?
- Does this reinforce good habits or bad ones?

[Use the Companion Guide to help you align your financial decisions with your goals.]

Now you have your overall financial vision and values. You have short-, intermediate-, and long-term goals, meaning you know where you're going. Plus, you have your financial snapshot involving your income, expenses, assets, and debt. That means you know where you are today.

This part of the book has helped you learn, plan, and execute a personal process for financial success. You developed a financial mind map that gave you a bird's-eye view of your financial picture, determining where you need to focus. Then, you overcame one of the biggest obstacles to financial success: mindless spending. After this, you looked at ways to make more money and made a SMARTER goal for boosting your income. This chapter introduced ways to break and replace financial habits and automate your financial decisions so that your financial success requires fewer decisions.

You have the tools in your hands now for mindful and intentional money management. If you take them and run with them, you'll have what you need to go from chaos to calm in your finances. It will be a journey. There will be tough decisions and difficult weeks ahead as you reduce your expenses, increase your income, reduce debt, and make wise investments. However, there is light at the end of the tunnel. You will soon find the entire process becoming more natural and peaceful, as your financial snapshot begins to resemble your financial goals.

Chapter Summary

Two key principles were discussed for making your success with finances inevitable: habits and automations. Like learning a new physical skill, it takes time and discomfort to gain muscle memory. Once you have it down, though, it happens naturally. It also requires fewer decisions, which means less fatigue for you. The concept of breaking and *replacing* bad habits for greater financial health was discussed. And finally, we discussed automations to make everything easier that will require less time for you with math calculations and building spreadsheets.

 KEY TAKEAWAYS

- Muscle memory will make financial decisions a habit, thus reducing decision fatigue.
- Replace expensive habits with sustainable new behaviors.
- Automate your spending, investments, and debt payments to reduce your time and effort in managing these decisions.

- If you have any of the vices I mentioned, consider reducing or replacing them. At minimum, include them in your financial planning.
- Take the mindful and intentional money management tools that you have learned in this book to move from financial chaos to calm.

ANCHORD
MONEY

CONCLUSION AND INVITATION

Your journey through this book is nearly at an end. A great deal of ground has been covered. In this final section, I want to recap what you've learned and invite you to continue the journey with me.

- Part 1: You looked at where you're going financially:
  - » Understanding where you're going financially was discussed. Your financial destination consists of learning your money habits, understanding how money impacts the most important areas of your life, and setting SMARTER goals for your money.
  - » Discovering your money habits meant diving deep into your behavior around money and where it comes from. You examined money scripts, beliefs, and perspectives on money that you may not have been aware of before. Then, you looked at your money personality, your default cluster of behaviors around money. This led to an exploration of your money habits, attitudes, and values.

» Following this, you looked at the eight areas of life that money impacts, and then looked at the ways they impact money. You discovered that as you begin improving in one of these aspects, the other areas tend to improve as well. This gave you the necessary information needed to set SMARTER goals. To be successful, these must be specific, measurable, achievable, relevant, time-bound, exciting, and recorded.

- Part 2: You looked at where you are today financially:
  » You built a financial snapshot out of your income vs. expenses, assets vs. debt, debt-to-income ratio, and net worth.
  » You examined strategies for improvement to ensure that your net worth is increasing.

- Part 3: You learned and planned a personal process for financial success:
  » This began by creating a mind map to get a snapshot of your financial picture.
  » You then examined the reality of emotional spending, how to identify triggers, and how to navigate working through those emotions.
  » This led into mindful and intentional spending in general. In my many years of teaching financial literacy, I've learned that budget leaks are the most common obstacle holding people back from their financial goals.
  » Then, you learned about a variety of methods to make more money. Regardless of where you start, increasing your income, even temporarily, can help you pay off debt and increase your net worth through invest-

ments. Therefore, a temporary season of making more money is a common part of many journeys to financial success.

» Finally, you learned about building muscle memory to make your future financial success automatic (and less painful). I want to make sure your plan works in the real world, not just on paper. This involves a process of examining your financial habits that bust your budget. Lastly, you looked at ways to automate your financial thinking to reduce the time and energy spent on decisions.

Now, you know where you're going, you know where you are, and you have the tools to execute a personal process for financial success. You must make the decision to start executing the process. I can't make the decision for you; only you can change your financial situation. I hope that throughout these pages, you've gained a powerful framework for doing just that.

I encourage you to immediately begin putting these concepts into practice. Don't simply close this book and let it be a source of nice inspiration and nothing more.

Though your journey through this book is ending, our journey together is far from over. As I mentioned at the very beginning, I don't want to leave you feeling inspired but without support. So I've created a multitude of resources available on my website for you to continue the journey toward financial success by engaging in a community. They include

- A website with valuable resources (Anchord.money)
- The social media community
- Online courses with audio lectures and Companion Guides

- Podcasts
- One-on-one or group coaching
- Tools to teach your children, or younger people in your life, money management skills
- Webinars

Best wishes to you in pursuing your mindful and intentional money management journey. Simply take one day at a time and be more conscientious about your money decisions and you will make great strides in improving your overall financial health.

I'm excited to hear from you about how you are growing toward being mindful and intentional with your money and moving from chaos to calm in your finances. If you ever need any help with this vital area, don't hesitate to reach out.

Here's to your best financial future,

Linda

ABOUT THE AUTHOR

Linda Simpson earned a PhD from the University of Illinois and has taught financial literacy since 1994 in a variety of situations and through different platforms, such as face-to-face and online university courses, webinars, workshops, and conference presentations. During that time, she's helped *thousands* of people of all ages and across all life stages to set goals and create simple financial plans that are sustainable to their lifestyle and spending behaviors.

Academically, she's won several teaching awards, her student evaluations are superior, and her courses are in high demand. She has conducted numerous research studies and provided her expertise on a variety of financial topics, such as financial goal setting, money and debt management, financial planning, credit, consumer behavior/spending patterns, home buying, risk management, student loan debt, and fraud, through webinars, publications, and professional presentations at the local, state, national, and international levels. Her academic background and experiences provide the foundation for her to help you make educated decisions about your personal financial well-being.

You will find her teaching style very effective as she breaks down the information into small, understandable components followed by action steps that help you learn, retain, and apply your knowledge. Her book, online courses and resources, and Companion Guides are all carefully designed so you can be successful in grasping the content on your own or using the additional resources that are available to help you develop your plan and stay on track. She hopes that you are able to take advantage of these valuable resources to continue your journey in building a solid financial foundation.

Here's to your best financial future!

TO ACCESS YOUR FREE COMPANION GUIDE

Go to https://resources.anchord.money/book-companion-guide

Or you can scan the QR code below using either the camera or open a QR code scanning app on your smartphone or tablet. Hold your device steady and position the QR code within the frame of the camera. Make sure that the QR code is fully visible and that the entire code is within the scanning area. The camera should focus on the code and automatically scan it. Otherwise, tap on the screen to focus the camera manually.

Complete the requested information on the form, both your Name and Email Address, and we will email you the Companion Guide.

A free ebook edition is available with the purchase of this book.

To claim your free ebook edition:

1. Visit MorganJamesBOGO.com
2. Sign your name CLEARLY in the space
3. Complete the form and submit a photo of the entire copyright page
4. You or your friend can download the ebook to your preferred device

Morgan James
BOGO™

A **FREE** ebook edition is available for you or a friend with the purchase of this print book.

CLEARLY SIGN YOUR NAME ABOVE

Instructions to claim your free ebook edition:
1. Visit MorganJamesBOGO.com
2. Sign your name CLEARLY in the space above
3. Complete the form and submit a photo of this entire page
4. You or your friend can download the ebook to your preferred device

Print & Digital Together Forever.

Snap a photo

Free ebook

Read anywhere

Printed in the USA
CPSIA information can be obtained
at www.ICGtesting.com
JSHW020021090324
58879JS00004B/56